GLACIER PARK'S BLACKFEET AND THE GREAT NORTHERN RAILWAY

DAVID R. BUTLER

AMERICA THROUGH TIME

America Through Time®
An imprint of Sutton Publishing Inc.
www.through-time.com

First published 2025

ISBN 978-1-63499-563-4

Typeset in 10pt on13pt Sabon
Printed and bound in the United States of America

ACKNOWLEDGMENTS

Historic photos used in this book come from a variety of sources. I have tried to be as specific as possible for each photo or image, and any errors in attribution are strictly my own. Sources, and their abbreviations, include BNSF, Burlington Northern and Santa Fe; GLAC or GNP, Glacier National Park; GNR, Great Northern Railway; LOC, Library of Congress; MHS, Montana Historical Society; MNHS, Minnesota Historical Society; NPS, National Park Service; OHSL, Oregon Historical Society Library; USGS, U.S. Geological Survey; umt, University of Montana (the lower case usage is as the university uses the abbreviation); and YUL, Yale University Library.

My thanks are extended to the good folks at Sutton Publishing, the editorial and publishing team that worked with me in creating this book, especially Alan Sutton, Kena Longabaugh Smith, and Josh Greenland. It is a pleasure to work with such professionals.

Finally, thanks as always to my friends and especially my family. They accompanied me on many visits to Glacier National Park and supported my enthusiasm and passion for all things Glacier National Park.

CONTENTS

Acknowledgments 3
Introduction 7

1 Before the Park 13
2 Louis B. Hill and the Creation of Glacier National Park 28
3 The Great Northern's Extensive Ad Campaign Using the Blackfeet 32
4 Photographers Illustrating the Blackfeet for the Great Northern Railway 43
5 Writers Sponsored by the Great Northern Railway 57
6 Great Northern-supported Artists Showcasing the Blackfeet 63
7 Blackfeet Public Appearances and Publicity Excursions 85
8 Chief Two Guns White Calf 106

Afterword: The Great Northern Railway and "Glacier Park's Blackfeet" 119
Endnotes 120
Bibliography 126

INTRODUCTION

This is a story of exploitation, paternalism, and capitalism, all at the expense of the Blackfeet people, that was initiated and fostered by the Great Northern Railway to boost tourism to their holdings in Glacier National Park, Montana. In order to understand the relationship among the railway, the Blackfeet, and Glacier National Park, and the effects of this relationship, it is first necessary to provide some background on the Blackfeet, the Great Northern Railway, and the creation of Glacier National Park.

Glacier National Park is located in northwest Montana, along the Canadian border south of portions of Alberta and British Columbia. Its eastern border forms the western border of the Blackfeet Indian Reservation, home to the U.S. members of the greater Blackfoot Confederacy comprised of indigenous people both north and south of the U.S.–Canadian border.

So, who are "the Blackfeet" described and discussed in this book? The Blackfoot people (note the difference in spelling) are comprised of several tribes, one of which is subdivided by the U.S.–Canadian border. North of the border in Canada, the three tribes include the Blackfoot or *Siksika* (also called the Northern Blackfoot), the Blood or *Kainai*, and the Peigan (*Piikuni*). South of the U.S.–Canadian border, this last tribe is spelled Piegan and *Pikuni* (sometimes spelled *Pikunni* or *Pikanni*). The Piegan/*Pikuni* comprise the Blackfeet Nation in the United States, and the majority of them live on the Blackfeet Reservation east of Glacier National Park. Thus, all Blackfeet (residents of the United States) are Blackfoot (members of the greater Blackfoot people), but not all Blackfoot are Blackfeet. Canadian tribal members are Blackfoot, U.S. members are Blackfeet. This book examines the relationship between the Montana Blackfeet of the late nineteenth and early twentieth centuries (up to approximately 1940), predominantly residents of the Blackfeet Reservation, and the Great Northern Railway and Glacier National Park.[1, 2, 3, 4, 5, 6]

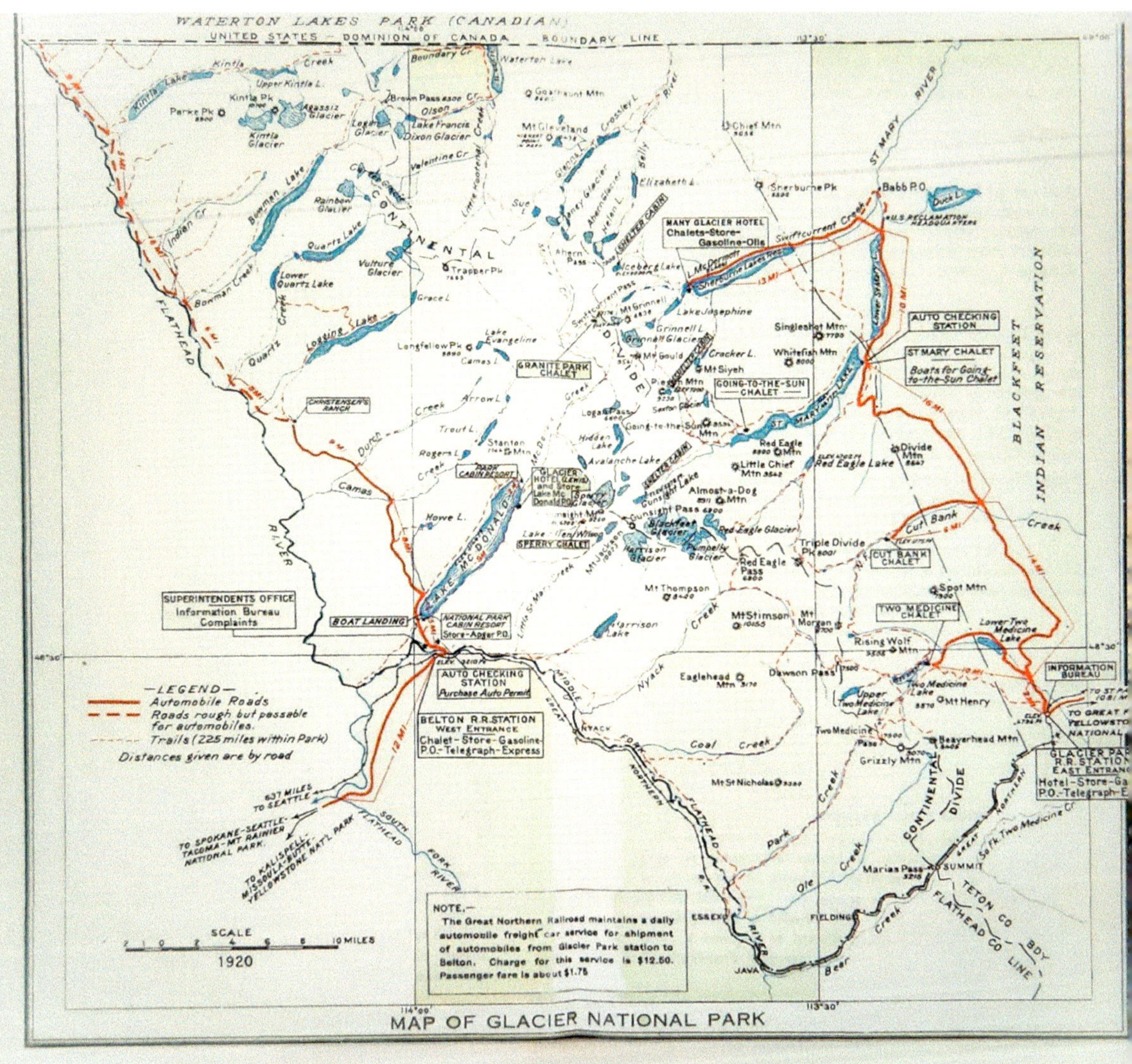

National Park Service map of Glacier National Park in 1920, illustrating the limited number of roads in existence during the early years of the park. Note that no road existed connecting Belton (West Glacier) and Glacier Park (East Glacier), no road existed from Apgar to the Glacier Hotel (today's Lake McDonald Lodge), and no Going-to-the-Sun Road existed linking Apgar with St. Mary. (*NPS*)

The location of the Blackfeet Reservation east of Glacier National Park, both bounded on the north by the Canadian border. Note the size of the reservation relative to the size of Glacier Park. (*USGS*)

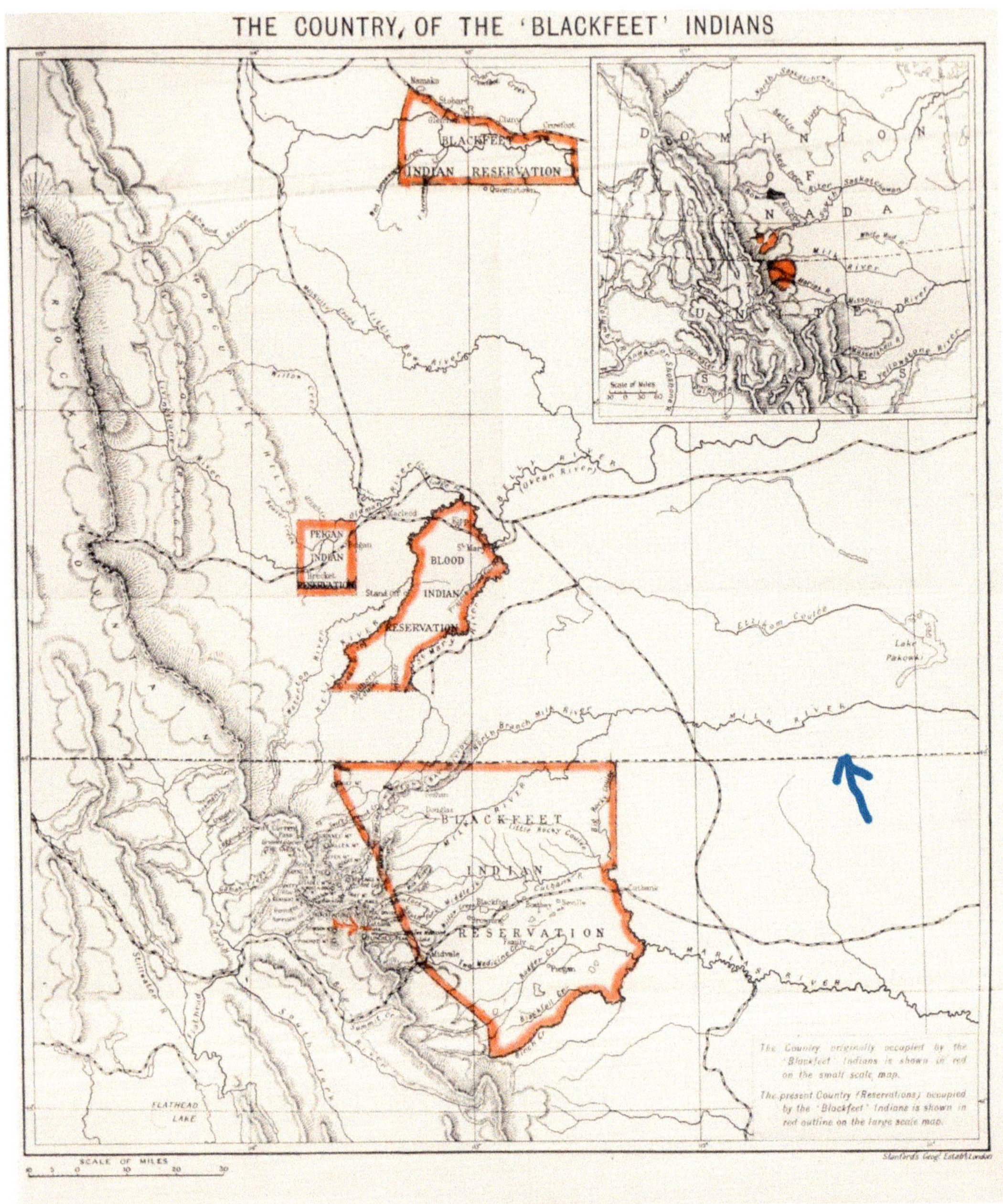

The location of the Blackfeet Reservation in northern Montana relative to the location of the additional reservations comprising the Blackfoot Confederacy in Canada. The blue arrow points to the U.S.–Canadian border. (*YUL WA MSS D1175 500, 401*)

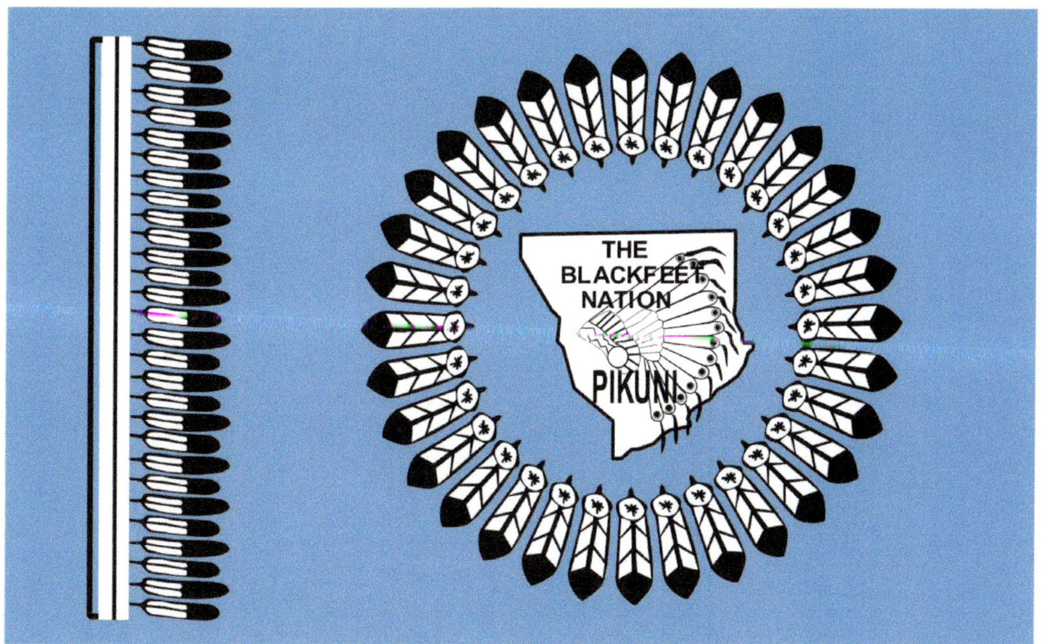

Flag of the Blackfeet Nation of Montana. The area in white within the black outline shows the shape of the Blackfeet Reservation. Also note the spelling of "Pikuni" on the flag. (*Wikipedia Commons*)

A final word or two of introduction is also in order. In this book, I refer to the Blackfeet as Native Americans or "indigenous people" wherever possible. Elsewhere in the text, I use the term "Indian" in "its historical context, while acknowledging that *Native American* (or in Canada, *First Nations*) is a more accurate and more respectful identifier of the people who inhabited the continent long before Europeans stepped ashore."[7]

Finally, the author of this book is a White Euro-American male, not a Native American. As historian Ryan Hall eloquently put it in his book on the Blackfoot People, "(a)s a non-Native person, I recognize that there are limits to my knowledge and my capacity to understand the nuances of Blackfoot culture.... I have therefore relied in large part on what might be called a 'colonial archive': documents written or mediated by outsiders like myself."[8] I apologize in advance for any mischaracterizations or misinterpretations of the Blackfeet people; such was most definitely not my intent.

1
BEFORE THE PARK

European Americans were in contact with the Blackfeet people for several decades before the creation of Glacier National Park in 1910. Weakened by smallpox outbreaks in 1789 and 1837, the Blackfeet population was in decline by the mid-nineteenth century, although they maintained a reputation as fierce warriors. The reduction and eventual disappearance by 1882 of the northern bison (incorrectly referred to as "buffalo") herd upon which the nomadic Blackfeet depended for food further weakened them. In 1855 (ratified in 1856), the Lame Bull Treaty provided the Blackfeet with a "guaranteed" homeland that was continuously whittled down in size over the next several decades. The Starvation Winter of 1883–1884 further reduced the population of the tribe, accounting for roughly 600 deaths. The reservation reached its current size in 1896 when a 20-mile swath of land on the western edge of the reservation, where Euro-Americans sought to exploit suspected mineral deposits, was ceded by the Blackfeet to the federal government for desperately needed cash. This so-called Ceded Strip forms the eastern half of today's Glacier National Park and remains a point of contention between the Blackfeet and the National Park Service. The Blackfeet claim they did not cede hunting, fishing, and grazing rights in the Ceded Strip, but the National Park Service (especially in the 1920s–1960s) insisted that such native rights were indeed ceded to the federal government.[1, 2]

Once a proud and feared people, by the latter half of the 1800s and the early 1900s, the Blackfeet were increasingly viewed by Euro-Americans with nostalgia as a culture facing potential extinction. This wistfulness concerning what was passing from the Montana landscape was reflected in the artistic works of several western artists, especially Cowboy Artist Charlie Russell, whose early days in Montana coincided with some of the worst times for the Blackfeet following the Starvation Winter. Russell deeply respected the Blackfeet and other Native American tribes, and his artwork attempted to memorialize the proud pre-Euro-American contact days of the Blackfeet (and other tribes).[3]

Left: The Blackfeet were exploited for commercial purposes long before Glacier Park and the Great Northern Railway existed. This advertising poster, for "Blackfoot Brand" cigars, dates from 1878. (*LOC 2022668187*)

Below: Cowboy artist Charles M. (Charlie) Russell regretted the loss of the Old West and painted his idealized version of Blackfeet life on the open prairie. This painting, *The Scouts*, completed in 1902, epitomizes his vision. (*C.M. Russell, public domain*)

When Sioux and Blackfeet Met is another of Charlie Russell's idealized versions of Blackfeet life prior to European–American contact. (*C.M. Russell, 1902 painting, LOC 99472673*)

For his several paintings of Blackfeet women, Charlie Russell utilized his non-Native American wife, Nancy Cooper Russell, as a life model. (*MHS p0003297, photographer unknown, 1897*)

Above: Keeoma 3, one of five Keeoma paintings by Russell, based on his wife's body modeling. The name Keeoma is derived from the Blackfeet word "kee-o-mee" or "kiomi," meaning "over there" or "yonder." (*C.M. Russell, 1898, MHS p0003297, public domain*)

Left: Charlie Russell dressed as a Blackfeet warrior, at Bull Head Lodge in Glacier National Park, where he frequently dressed in Native American garb. (*Photo by A.J. Thiri, 1916, umt015995*)

The completion of the Great Northern Railway across Montana in the early 1890s (it reached Spokane, Washington, in 1892 and Seattle in 1893) allowed eastern Euro-American artists, eager to nostalgically document what many viewed as the probable passing of a people, relatively easy access to the Blackfeet people and lands. Chief among these artists were photographers now renowned for their romantic, pictorialist views of indigenous cultures—Edward Curtis and Walter McClintock. Both photographers concentrated on illustrating a romantic, proud way of life they felt was rapidly disappearing, rather than documenting the poverty and distress that typified the Reservation during this period.[4]

Photographer Edward S. Curtis (1868–1952) was a well-known portrait photographer based out of Seattle, Washington. In 1899, Curtis was hired as a photographer for the Harriman Alaska Expedition based on his successful exhibition of local Native American photographs he displayed for the National Photographic Society. He was also a successful and accomplished mountain climber and outdoorsman, and he looked forward to being able to photograph Native Americans in the Alaskan region.[5]

On the Alaskan expedition, Edward Curtis renewed his acquaintanceship with another expedition member, who was perhaps America's foremost ethnographer of Plains Native Americans, George Bird Grinnell. Grinnell was well known for his friendships with and publications about the Blackfeet (as well as the Cheyenne), having first visited the area of what would become Glacier National Park in the fall of 1885. The Great Northern Railway did not yet extend across the Blackfeet Reservation at that time, and Grinnell reached the reservation via stagecoach from Helena. There, he met with his guide, James Willard Schultz, a Euro-American who had married into the Blackfeet tribe. Schultz had also written a series of articles for the *Forest and Stream* magazine (precursor to today's *Field and Stream*) which Grinnell first wrote for, then edited, and eventually owned. Schultz and Grinnell explored the St. Mary and Swiftcurrent valleys and became fast friends. Schultz also was Grinnell's mentor into the world of the Blackfeet to which Grinnell returned as often as possible, and subsequently Grinnell would act in the same fashion as a mentor into the world of the Blackfeet for Edward Curtis.[6]

Self portrait of photographer Edward S. Curtis, 1899. (*Smithsonian Institution, National Portrait Gallery, NPG.77.49*)

Upon completion of the Harriman Alaska Expedition of 1899, Grinnell invited Curtis to join him for a visit to the Blackfeet Reservation in July 1900 to experience the Blackfeet Medicine Lodge ceremony, also known as the Blackfeet Sun Dance. Curtis accepted the invitation and thus became one of the first prominent photographers whose visit to the Blackfeet Reservation was facilitated by the Great Northern Railway. With Grinnell as his introduction to Blackfeet society, Curtis took portraits of several prominent Blackfeet chiefs as well as the Medicine Lodge. He also, however, took numerous romantic, posed photos of the Blackfeet in "natural settings—beside a river, seated in a lodge, on horseback. His conscientious treatment evoked a golden age, not quite past but nearly so."[7] Such photographs became Curtis' trademark, and formed the foundation for his *magnum opus*, the magnificent twenty-volume *The North American Indian* published over the period 1907 to 1930, containing over 2,000 photos from eighty tribes and locations across the American West. Most of Curtis' photographs of the Blackfeet do not show much of the scenery of Glacier National Park but concentrate on the individuals being photographed. Nonetheless, Curtis' Blackfeet images tied them in the public mind to the general landscape of what would become Glacier National Park, and these images would have been extremely difficult to achieve without the presence of the Great Northern Railway's ability to deliver Curtis (and Grinnell) to the reservation.[8]

Walter McClintock (1870–1946) was born in Pittsburgh, PA, and attended Yale University from 1887 to his graduation in 1891. In 1895, he took a trip through parts of North Dakota, Montana, Idaho, and Wyoming, during which he became enamored of the western region and western life. In 1896, McClintock took the Great Northern to the Blackfeet Reservation to join the National Forest Commission as a photographer, led by another Yale graduate, Gifford Pinchot (Pinchot would go on to become the first head of the U.S. Forest Service). McClintock actually had little photography experience at that time but took advantage of his Yale connections to secure the position.[9]

McClintock, through his duties as photographer for the National Forest Commission, slowly became enamored with the Blackfeet people. After three weeks with the commission in the general environs of what would become Glacier National Park, he left the commission group with guide William "Billy" Jackson, a mixed-blood scout and guide fluent in the Blackfeet language. McClintock spent several months with Jackson, primarily along the eastern front of the mountains in the general area of Cut Bank Creek. Jackson introduced McClintock to numerous Blackfeet, and through Jackson, McClintock met a prominent Blackfeet elder and leading chief, Mad Wolf. Jackson acted as linguistic intermediary for the other two men, and Mad Wolf would eventually adopt McClintock as his "white son" in the summer of 1898 during McClintock's second visit to the reservation. He would return numerous times thereafter, particularly between 1898 and 1910, and eventually took over 2,000 photographs of the Blackfeet, many of which he had hand-colorized in support of his public lectures on the tribe. He also studied their music and way of life and became a well-respected ethnographer of the tribe. He wrote of his time among the Blackfeet and his adoption by Mad Wolf in his autobiographical book *The Old North Trail*, published in 1920. His photographs of the Blackfeet are very pictorialist in nature, evoking a nostalgic view of the tribe and their life prior to the desperate times of the late 1800s.[10, 11]

Piegan encampment with the southern mountains of what would become Glacier National Park in the background, Summit Mountain on far left. (*Edward S. Curtis photo, circa 1900, LOC 90707595*)

Above left: Young Piegan woman wearing beaded dress and posed in a pastoral setting, *circa* 1910. (*Edward S. Curtis photo, LOC 92520029*)

Above right: Flint Smoker's daughter, *circa* 1910. (*Edward S. Curtis photo, LOC 94514250*)

Above left: "The Grizzly Bear, Piegan," *circa* 1910. (*Edward S. Curtis photo, LOC 93504353*)

Above right: Piegan woman, *circa* 1910. (*Edward S. Curtis photo, LOC 96501716*)

Left: Photographer Walter McClintock dressed in Native American regalia at Southwest Museum, *circa* 1940. (*Photographer unknown, public domain photo*)

Walter McClintock on the rear deck of the Great Northern Railway's *Oriental Limited* observation car, *circa* 1905–1911. This picture typifies the influence the Great Northern had in impacting the Blackfeet people—the Great Northern offered McClintock and others the fastest access existing at that time to the Blackfeet Reservation. (*Photographer unknown, hand-tinted by Charlotte M. Pinkerton, YUL WA MSS S1175 202*)

Walter McClintock and Brings Down the Sun, summer 1905. (*Photographer unknown, YUL WA MSS S1175 G540.2*)

"Calf Tail of the Blackfoot people, his wife [Different Gun Woman], their daughter Cecil[e] Calf Tail, and the two wives of Running Rabbit standing outside a painted tipi. Calf Tail holds a spear and his wife holds a hand drum." (*Walter McClintock photo, circa 1905–1915, MHS p0002811*)

Above left: "Blackfoot girl." (*Walter McClintock photo, undated, YUL WA MSS S1175 GS-130*)

Above right: Hand-tinted version of "Blackfoot girl." (*Walter McClintock photo, undated, tinting by Charlotte M. Pinkerton, YUL WA MSS S1175 Y-1432*)

View west across prairie with snow to southern peaks of Glacier National Park, May 1906. (*Walter McClintock photo, YUL WA MSS S1175 F6185*)

"Tipis on the prairie," *circa* 1910. The view is northwestward to Divide Mountain at left-center. (*Walter McClintock photo, hand-tinted by Charlotte M. Pinkerton, YUL WA MSS S1175 1044*)

Closer view of the camp shown in the previous hand-tinted picture, summer 1909. Divide Mountain is the triangle-shaped peak near center. (*Walter McClintock photo, hand-tinted by Annette Karge, YUL WA MSS S1175 1074*)

Opposite above: Cut Bank Canyon Camp. (*Walter McClintock photo, circa 1910, YUL WA MSS S1175 G700*)

Opposite below: "Camp Parade," summer 1909. View westward to Divide Mountain at right-center, and the flat summit of East Flattop Mountain at far right. (*Walter McClintock photo, YUL WA MSS S1175 G873a*)

Undated poster advertising presentations by Walter McClintock based on his time among the Blackfeet people. (*YUL MSS S1175 Box 9, folder 253-257*)

The Great Northern *Flyer* crossing the Two Medicine River bridge east of Glacier Park Station, summer 1905. (*Walter McClintock photo, YUL WA MSS S1175 G508*)

The Two Medicine River Bridge, July 21, 2012. (*Photo by author*)

2

LOUIS B. HILL AND THE CREATION OF GLACIER NATIONAL PARK

The role of Louis B. Hill in assisting with the creation of Glacier National Park is shrouded somewhat in mystery. It is well documented that "The Father of Glacier National Park" was the conservationist, author, and ethnographer George Bird Grinnell, who worked tirelessly to lobby legislators in Congress to write and pass legislation authorizing the creation of a national park, which eventually succeeded and culminated in the passing of legislation by Congress signed by President William Howard Taft on May 11, 1910. Hill, who succeeded his father James J. Hill (the founder) as president of the Great Northern Railway in 1907, chose a less public role, in order to avoid the specter of having a commercial entity, the railway, publicly advocating for the creation of a park. Hill chose to avoid such a seemingly obvious conflict of interest and therefore avoided any correspondence with Grinnell about working for the creation of Glacier Park. Instead, Hill sent behind-the-scenes telegrams to members of Congress urging their support for the legislation. Nonetheless, in his later years, Grinnell noted that the Great Northern Railway (and by extension, Louis Hill) had influence with Montana senators and that the railway had been "made to see the possibilities of the region."[1, 2, 3]

Upon its creation in May 1910, Hill immediately set an ambitious plan into motion to make the new Glacier National Park a premiere tourist destination for wealthy easterners and mid-westerners who would need to take Hill's Great Northern Railway to reach this new scenic wonder. Hill's two-pronged plan, which has earned him the nickname from some of "the Godfather of Glacier Park" was to relentlessly publicize the park in two ways: 1) tout the park as "The Switzerland of America," in concert with the railway's extensive "See America First" campaign, with the slogan plastered underneath the railway logo on freight cars across the country; and 2) tie into the public's mind the close relationship between Glacier National Park and the Blackfeet tribe, such that they became virtually synonymous and indistinguishable from each other. If a tourist chose to come to see Glacier Park, they also were choosing to come and see the Blackfeet people. Hill effectively created, in the public's mind, the "Glacier Park Indians." This selling point of Native Americans intimately linked together with a scenic national park was something that neither the Northern Pacific Railway had available for its promotions of Yellowstone National Park, nor the Santa Fe Railway in their promotions for their branch railroad from Williams, Arizona, to Grand Canyon National Park.[4]

In order to attract wealthy tourists to the new national park, tourism infrastructure was required. Hill saw that the federal government was providing almost no financial support for the new park, and so devoted serious capital for the development of such infrastructure. He developed the plan for a series of Swiss-chalet-themed hotels and chalets distributed a day's horseback-ride apart along the eastern front of the new park, beginning at the Great Northern Railway station in Midvale, soon renamed as Glacier Park and extending northward; as well as a similar Swiss-themed chalet at the train station on the western side of the park in Belton. Chalets were built at Belton, Two Medicine, Cut Bank, St. Mary, Sun Point (Going-to-the-Sun Chalets), Many Glacier, Gunsight Lake, Sperry, and Granite Park. The Belton Chalet was the first Great Northern Facility opened in the park, adjacent to the Belton railroad station in what is now West Glacier (although the station retains the name Belton), opening barely a month after the Park's creation, on June 27, 1910.[5, 6, 7, 8, 9]

The centerpiece of Hill's vision for developing Glacier Park and providing accommodations was Glacier Park Lodge (called Glacier Park Hotel in its early days) in the village of East Glacier Park (then called Glacier Park, after being first renamed from the original village name Midvale). The lodge and the suite of chalet groups opened for the summer season of 1913. In 1914, the Great Northern subsidiary company, the Glacier Park Hotel Company, was created to manage this burgeoning set of tourist accommodations. Hill also envisioned and directed the creation of the Many Glacier Hotel completed in 1915 in the Swiftcurrent Valley, and the Prince of Wales Hotel in adjacent Waterton Lakes National Park, Alberta, in 1927. Hill had his own summer cabin complex built on a point of land jutting out into St. Mary Lake, just up the lake from Sun Point and the Going-to-the-Sun Chalets.[10]

Above: Louis W. Hill, president of the Great Northern Railway, at Glacier Park Lodge *circa* 1913–1920. (*Photo by Morton J. Elrod, GLAC HPF 1950*)

Left: The Great Northern Railway logo on the side of a railroad boxcar, illustrating its constant advertisement for Glacier National Park. (*Photo by Jack Delano, March 1943. LOC 2017849186*)

Right: Louis W. Hill with Chief Two Guns White Calf in Glacier National Park, 1925. The location is unspecified but the scenery in the rear looks like the view from Sun Point. (*Photographer uncredited, Minnesota Historical Society*)

Below: Going-to-the-Sun Chalets on Sun Point, St. Mary Lake, Glacier Park, *circa* 1920s–1930s. Louis W. Hill's cabin complex was located on the rocky point of land at right center jutting out into the lake, above the roof of the chalet on the far right. (*T.J. Hileman photo, GLAC 5229*)

3

THE GREAT NORTHERN'S EXTENSIVE AD CAMPAIGN USING THE BLACKFEET

With his Swiss-themed infrastructure underway in the park, Hill moved to imprint in the public's mind the significance of the Blackfeet tribe as an integral component of the Glacier Park experience. With visitors arriving from the east at Glacier Park Station, located on the Blackfeet Reservation only a few hundred steps from his showpiece Glacier Park Lodge, Hill was provided the perfect stage for re-casting the Blackfeet as a colorful, peaceful component of the Glacier Park experience. His plan included: put the Blackfeet on display in Glacier Park (East Glacier) where tourists arrived via the Great Northern; advertise and widely brand that the Blackfeet were "Glacier Park's Indians" and publish a diversity of postcards, pamphlets, booklets, and other marketing items making this link commonplace in the public mind; and send out representative Blackfeet on public relation tours and appearances at important events across the country, where the tribal members put on cultural displays and encouraged the public to "come visit them in Glacier Park." Louis Hill did pay the Blackfeet what was, for the time, a fair wage for their services in East Glacier and around Glacier Park and on tour. However, Hill's vision of how to present the Blackfeet to the public was somewhat at odds with the truth as well as the tribe's proud history. Hill's version of the Blackfeet was a friendly and peaceful people eager to meet with the tourist public. He required the Blackfeet to abandon their own upright war bonnets (styled somewhat like a beef standing rib roast) for the more well-known Sioux bonnets that flowed down their backs. In general, their "genuine" clothing seen by the tourists was Hill's "Hollywood" version of what Euro-Americans believed Native Americans should look like, rather than authentic Blackfeet cultural representations.[1]

Visitors arriving at Glacier Park were greeted by Blackfeet tribal members in full "authentic" regalia at the train station. During their walk from the station up to the Glacier Park Lodge, the visitors would pass a "genuine Indian village" of pitched Blackfeet tepees. Blackfeet were present to greet the visitors. At the Lodge in the evenings, Blackfeet tribal members would put on programs about the tribe, demonstrate dances and songs, and mingle with guests.[2, 3]

Glacier Park Lodge in Glacier Park (East Glacier), on the Blackfeet Reservation, 1914. Note the numerous Blackfeet lodges between the entrance portico to the hotel grounds and the hotel. (*Photo by Harris and Ewing, LOC 2016864826*)

In addition to the on-site Blackfeet experience for visitors to Glacier Park Lodge and station, the Great Northern Railway's publicity department, at Louis Hill's direction, cranked out massive amounts of publicity concerning the Blackfeet and their relationship with Glacier National Park. "Fully half of the promotion for Glacier Park featured the Blackfeet who were always identified as 'the Glacier Park Indians'."[3] Pamphlets and booklets about the Blackfeet and their seemingly close ties with the park were widely distributed by the railway, as were promotional flyers, postcards, luggage tags, and other paraphernalia. The Great Northern lodges were decorated with Blackfeet symbology, for which publicity booklets explaining the symbology were distributed.[4, 5, 6, 7, 8, 9]

Nor was the publicity department for the railway constrained by the truth. They created, out of thin air, Blackfeet women working at tasks they likely never actually performed. The most egregious example of lies created by the Great Northern's publicity machine was "Princess Dawn Mist" (sometimes referred to as "Queen of the Blackfeet"), who was featured on postcards as well as on promotional tours. The part of Princess Dawn Mist was, at least in a hat tip to the truth, played by young Blackfeet women, first by Daisy M. Norris in the 1910s.[10]

> She was hired to pose as Princess Dawn Mist by Great Northern publicist Hoke Smith, who created the fictional persona of Princess Dawn Mist, drawing from Helen Fitzgerald Sander's novel and wrote stories about her that circulated across the country in newspapers hungry for information about the "Wild West" and its real Native American tribes. The public did not know that the individuals involved in Smith's stories, including Princess Dawn Mist, were completely fictional, designed to further imprint in the public mind the connection between Glacier Park and the Blackfeet.

Blackfeet tribal member Irene Goss replaced Daisy Norris Gilham as Princess Dawn Mist sometime in the 1920s. As Dawn Mist, Goss went on extensive tours with roughly three dozen Blackfeet tribal members to major cities throughout the northeastern and midwestern United States, and was "the face" of the touring group.[11]

An example of the Blackfeet-centric advertising campaign carried out by the Great Northern Railway in their ads for enticing visitors to Glacier National Park, in this case from a 1925 multi-page booklet. (*Great Northern Railway, author's personal collection*)

Above: Examples of Blackfeet-oriented advertising and artwork touting the relationship between the Blackfeet and Glacier National Park, from a display in the Glacier Park Station railroad terminal in East Glacier Park. (*Photo by author, July 21, 2012*)

Right: An example of a promotional Great Northern Railway-sponsored postcard touting the relationship between the Blackfeet people and Glacier National Park, here on the shore of Two Medicine Lake. (*Great Northern Railway photo, undated; author's personal collection*)

"Princess Dawn Mist" and Chief Wolf Robe in Glacier National Park, probably along either the St. Mary River or Cut Bank Creek where similar photos were taken, in a promotional colorized postcard circulated by the Great Northern Railway. (*Great Northern Railway photo undated, photo unattributed but probably taken by Roland Reed*)

Two versions of the same photo of "Princess Dawn Mist," taken in 1915. The right-hand photo was hand-colored and sold as a postcard, and on it Dawn Mist has been "promoted" from a Blackfeet Princess to "Queen of the Blackfeet." (*Photos in public domain, but from GNR and taken by Roland Reed*)

Two photos of Dawn Mist, as played by Daisy M. Gilham. Left, unattributed photo taken 1914; right, postcard photo (note GNR logo in lower right, and bottom line of caption reads "Glacier National Park, Montana—See America First") taken *circa* 1912–1915. (*Left, public domain photo; right, GNR, photo by Roland Reed, University of Washington Libraries Special Collections Division*)

Evidence that Louis Hill's campaign to brand the Blackfeet as "Glacier Park/Park's Indians" was a raging success, this recording from May 23, 1914, preserves the voices of Blackfeet people singing two tribal songs. A third song, "Medicine Song," is preserved on a separate recording and also attributed to "Glacier Park Indians." (*LOC 17611*)

Blackfeet pictorial writing is illustrated in this *circa* 1914 photograph. The Great Northern Railway identified the artists of such works as "The Blackfeet Indians of Glacier National Park," and had forty-two individual picture-writing panels created by Blackfeet artists on the walls of Glacier Park Lodge (twelve panels), Many Glacier Hotel (twenty panels), and Going-to-the-Sun Chalets (ten panels). The meanings of each panel were described in a 1920 booklet published by the Great Northern's Glacier Park Hotel Company, and a colorized version of this picture graced the cover of that publication. (*Photo unattributed, LOC 95508628*)

A posed publicity photo, attributed to the Great Northern Railway, purportedly showing "Helen of Many Glacier" working as a telephone switchboard operator at the Many Glacier Hotel, June 26, 1925. Unfortunately, no evidence exists that any Blackfeet person was employed at the Many Glacier Hotel during that time, and it is unlikely that the young woman's name was Helen. (*Bain News Service, LOC 2014718418*)

Another possibly posed publicity-style photo of Mrs. Many Horse, working at a typewriter and stretching her chewing gum with her left hand. (*Undated and unattributed photo, LOC 2003665487*)

More information about the Blackfeet publicity tours mentioned above is provided in this book in Chapters 7 and 8. Here, I will present an example from one of the earliest Blackfeet publicity tours at a time when the Great Northern publicity engine was still learning how best to market the "Glacier Park Indians."

In March 1913, Louis Hill arranged for a special car of the Great Northern Railway to bring a contingent of Blackfeet to the Travel and Vacation Show, held at the Grand Central Palace in New York City. The tribal members were put up at the Hotel McAlpin on Herald Square. The publicity people for the railroad floated a completely false story that the Blackfeet refused to sleep indoors and insisted on pitching their tepees on the roof of the hotel. The tribal members did indeed pitch tepees on the hotel roof, strictly for publicity purposes, but they did not sleep in them, instead taking advantage of the comfortable rooms offered by the hotel and sleeping inside like other customers. Thousands of visitors as well as the press were cordially received by the Blackfeet atop the hotel roof during their stay from March 20–29, but the fallacy of them refusing to sleep inside was strictly a publicity stunt and outright lie perpetrated by the railway. The success of this publicity lie buoyed the confidence of the publicity arm of the railroad, and many more lies would follow. Among the ten members of the tribe brought to New York City were Chief Three Bears (one of the elder tribal members) and Chief Two Guns White Calf, son of Chief White Calf who was one of the tribal members who negotiated the treaty that ceded reservation land (with controversies that exist to the present day as to the rights of the Blackfeet therein) for what is now the eastern half of Glacier National Park to the federal government.[12]

Chief Two Guns White Calf worked for the Great Northern Railway and travelled widely to popularize Glacier National Park. The Great Northern circulated the rumor that he was the model for the early twentieth-century "Buffalo Nickel" coin; that claim has been discredited, but the railway, in a blatant example of their creating facts from thin air, continued to perpetuate it nonetheless. (*Undated Bain News Service photo, LOC 2006684403*)

Right: Chief Two Guns White Calf on the roof of the Hotel McAlpin in New York City, March 1913, during a publicity tour of ten Blackfeet tribal members sponsored by Louis W. Hill as part of the Glacier National Park exhibit at the Travel and Vacation Show at the Grand Central Palace. Over 10,000 visitors a day visited White Calf and his colleagues from March 20–29, 1913, during their residence at the hotel. (*Byron Company photo, Collections of the Museum of the City of New York*)

Below: The visiting Blackfeet tribal members posing on the roof of the Hotel McAlpin, New York City, March 1913. (*Byron Company photo, Collections of the Museum of the City of New York*)

The visiting Blackfeet tribal members gaze upon New York City from the roof of the Hotel McAlpin. The lodge/tepee shown was a publicity stunt, the Blackfeet stayed in rooms in the hotel. (*Byron Company photo, Collections of the Museum of the City of New York*)

The visiting Blackfeet look over New York City, Two Guns White Calf is fourth from the left. (*Byron Company photo, Collections of the Museum of the City of New York*)

4

PHOTOGRAPHERS ILLUSTRATING THE BLACKFEET FOR THE GREAT NORTHERN RAILWAY

As the Great Northern Railway began to market Glacier National Park after its creation in 1910, they realized that visual publicity was the key for enticing visitors to come to the new park. Visual publicity in the 1910–1940 period meant postcards, newspaper and magazine advertising, pamphlets and brochures (examined in Chapter 3), and book illustrations, all of which required photographs and artwork. This chapter examines the photographers and their creations that illustrated not only the new national park, but the relationship between Glacier Park and the Blackfeet (whether accurately displayed or not). Chapters 5 and 6 examine the way in which books (Chapter 5) and artists (Chapter 6) were employed by the railroad to indelibly create the linkage between Glacier Park and the Blackfeet tribe in the public mind.

Fred Kiser

Fred Kiser was born in 1878 in Grand Island, Nebraska, but while very young his parents moved to Warrendale, Oregon, in the scenic Columbia River gorge east of Portland. He and his brother, Oscar, grew up in this scenic setting and began to take and sell photographs of the gorge landscape. In 1904, Fred worked as the official photographer for the Louisiana Purchase 100-year-anniversary exposition, in St. Louis, Missouri. His work there led to him being named official photographer for the 1905 Lewis and Clark Centennial Exposition in Portland. His work there caught the attention of Louis Hill of the Great Northern Railway, who became president of the railroad in 1907.[1]

One of the unique aspects of Fred Kiser's photography was his development and creation of "artographs," a process using hand coloring of black-and-white photographs with transparent photo oils. This process allowed for the creation of artificial "color" photographs. The sale of his colored artographs made Kiser's work even more popular.

How accurately the hand-coloring depicted the actual colors of the photographed landscape is open to interpretation. Louis Hill didn't care, he wanted artographs to support his efforts to have the Glacier Park region declared a national park. Hill therefore hired Kiser in 1909, which began a six-year relationship between Kiser and the Great Northern.[2, 3]

The Great Northern provided Kiser with his own boxcar which he used as quarters and a "rolling studio," and he began photographing the area before it became a national park. Louis Hill used over 100 of Kiser's colorful artograph prints in the Capitol building in Washington, D.C., with this exhibit credited with providing the final push for Congressional approval for establishing Glacier National Park in 1910.[4]

Fred Kiser's photos show Glacier Park in its earliest years. By 1915, he and the railway had parted ways, in a dispute over copyright ownership of his photos. Although a number of his photos showed Blackfeet tribal members that the railway used to exploit the relationship between the new park and the railway, Kiser's photos are predominantly known for their outstanding scenic beauty illustrating the Glacier Park landscape. Numerous examples of his scenic works can be found elsewhere.[5, 6]

Great Northern photographer Fred Kiser poses with his unnamed cook, showcasing Kiser's Great Northern "Photographic Special Car 1000, 'Kiser' Official Photographer," *circa* 1910. The location of the photograph is unspecified. (*Photographer unknown, OHSL ba021218*)

Right: Fred Kiser photo of Chief Two Guns White Calf, 1912. Note the linking of Two Guns White Calf with Glacier National Park rather than with the Blackfeet Reservation. (*GNP Archives 78376*)

Below: Colorized Fred Kiser photo, *circa* 1910, of a Blackfeet camp near the outlet of St. Mary Lake in Glacier National Park. Singleshot Mountain is the peak at upper left. (*OHSL ba021222*)

Roland Reed

Whereas Fred Kiser was known primarily for his scenic photographs that, in some instances, included the Blackfeet, photographer Roland Reed became well known for his photos of Native Americans, including the Blackfeet, that also happened to show the scenic beauty in which the tribe lived. Reed the pictorialist was less interested in recording an image or scene as it was but rather attempted to recreate how he believed (or wished) the Blackfeet lived prior to European contact. Reed's primary period of photography in and adjacent to Glacier Park on the Blackfeet Reservation was from 1909 to 1915, during which time he opened and operated a photography studio in nearby Kalispell, Montana. His images, like other pictorialists such as Edward Curtis, were typically staged, with the Blackfeet posing in locations where they quite possibly did not belong, in reconstructed tribal dress as envisioned by Reed, not authentic Blackfeet tribal dress.[7]

During his period of activity in Glacier Park, Reed contracted with the Great Northern Railway to provide artistic photos of the Blackfeet for their campaign of branding into the public mind the relationship between the Blackfeet and the Park. Reed also took photographs of the famous author of Blackfeet stories, James Willard Schultz, in 1915 for use in Schultz' 1916 Great Northern-sponsored book, *Blackfeet Tales of Glacier National Park* (see next chapter). Other photos by Reed eventually also appeared in several other books, most notably Agnes Laut's *Enchanted Trails of Glacier Park*, a book also sponsored by the Great Northern.[8, 9, 10]

Portrait of Roland Reed, well-known pictorialist photographer of Native Americans, in Kalispell, Montana, *circa* 1912. (*Undated, public domain photo*)

One of Roland Reed's most famous Blackfeet photos, "The Eagle," at Sun Point on St. Mary Lake, photo taken between 1910 and 1915. Copies of this image are to this day still sold at numerous shops in St. Mary and East Glacier. (*R. Reed photo, Wikipedia Commons*)

Piegan tribal member on a horse with travois, near the mouth of the Cut Bank Valley in Glacier National Park, Montana, between 1912 and 1915. This and several other Reed photos were published as postcards, in the "See America First" Great Northern Railway National Park Route photogravure series. (*Roland Reed photo, University of Washington Libraries, Special Collections Division AWC4280*)

Blackfeet encampment, St. Mary Lake, 1916. (*R. Reed photo, GNP Archives 670971*)

"The Beaver Dam" shows three Blackfeet braves looking for beaver sign at a beaver dam on the shore of Swiftcurrent Lake. Photo taken prior to the completion of the Many Glacier Hotel in 1915. (*R. Reed photo, from J. W. Schultz's book Blackfeet Tales of Glacier National Park, book in author's personal collection*)

Similar view to the previous picture, looking across Swiftcurrent Lake, frozen in this winter view. The Many Glacier Hotel now dominates the far shoreline of the lake. (*Photo by author, February 6, 1995*)

R. E. "Ted" Marble

Ted Marble essentially stepped into the shoes vacated by Fred Kiser, becoming a scenic photographer of Glacier Park for the Great Northern Railway. Although he began working in 1913 until his enlistment in the U.S. Army for deployment in World War I, his work from that period is little known because he did not receive credit for his photos. After his return from the army in 1919, he began to receive credit from the railway for his photos, and as a result became much more well known. Marble opened a photography studio in Whitefish, Montana, in 1923, where he sold photos of scenic landscapes and photographed local residents. He continued to operate in Glacier Park periodically until his death. Marble's photos, like Kiser's, concentrated on scenery rather than on the Blackfeet; accordingly, distinctly fewer Marble photos of the Blackfeet exist, but those that do offer excellent scenic displays yet again confirming for the public the relationship between Glacier Park and the Blackfeet tribe.[11]

Blackfeet braves posing in front of Running Eagle Falls in the Two Medicine Valley in Glacier Park, 1917. (*R. Marble photo, MHS p0009170*)

R. Marble photo of Glacier Park Lodge, 1920, with Blackfeet lodges on the hotel lawn. (*GNP Archives*)

T. J. Hileman

Tomar Jacob "T. J." Hileman's career in landscape photography "took off" when he was appointed the official photographer for the Great Northern Railway in 1925, succeeding R. E. "Ted" Marble in that capacity. The railway paid Hileman $125 per month, for which payment Hileman pursued landscape views with abandon, carrying a heavy box camera and tripod equipment to precarious perches all over the park, earning him the nickname "Mountain Goat" Hileman. Hileman also took photographs of the Blackfeet, assisting the continuation of the Great Northern's campaign to make the Blackfeet synonymous with Glacier Park in the public mind. Unlike Fred Kiser and Ted Marble before him, Hileman negotiated a deal with the Great Northern that allowed him to retain copyright ownership of his images, although the railway could purchase copies for 35 cents per print to use in their promotional materials. This ownership of his photos allowed Hileman to sell to postcard companies, which reproduced his images widely. Like Fred Kiser before him, Hileman's photos were also used as illustrations in a number of popular tourist-available books. He produced iconic photos of numerous locations throughout Glacier National Park, as well as photos of the Blackfeet people on that landscape. Unlike Kiser or Marble, Hileman took a number of portrait photos of Blackfeet tribal members, including a striking and well-known photo of Chief Two Guns White Calf (see more about Two Guns in Chapter 8).[12]

Great Northern photographer T. J. Hileman's photo of Chief Chewing Blackbones, May 1933. (*umt010574*)

Left: Hileman photo of Chief Two Guns White Calf, *circa* 1920s. (*MHS p0002769*)

Below: Chief Two Guns White Calf on the shore of Swiftcurrent Lake in the Many Glacier Valley, with Mt. Wilbur directly behind him, *circa* 1913–1918. (*T. J. Hileman photo, public domain*)

Mrs. Louise Beery Child at Glacier Park Lodge, *circa* 1924–1935. (*T. J. Hileman photo, MHS p0002774*)

Postcard photo of Arrow Top Knot on a rocky outcrop in the Many Glacier Valley, *circa* 1930s. (*T. J. Hileman photo, MHS p0002718*)

5
WRITERS SPONSORED BY THE GREAT NORTHERN RAILWAY

The Great Northern Railway publicity machine covered as many bases as possible. In addition to photographers producing images linking the Blackfeet people with the landscape of Glacier National Park in the public's mind, the railroad also hired popular writers who produced books and articles forging the same links for the public. Several of these writers had long histories with the Glacier Park area from the pre-park era into the 1930s era. Among the most significant of these authors were James Willard Schultz, George Bird Grinnell, Walter McClintock, and Mary Roberts Rinehart. Because much of their efforts related to the park, the railway, and the Blackfeet occurred in pre-Park days, Grinnell and McClintock were examined in Chapter 2 of this book. Schultz and Rinehart are discussed below. Other Great Northern-sponsored writers included Grace Flandrau, Agnes Laut, and Margaret Thompson, each associated with significant historical publications about aspects of Glacier Park and its affiliation with the Blackfeet people. These three authors have been previously discussed elsewhere.[1, 2, 3, 4, 5]

James Willard Schultz

James Willard Schultz is among the most famous names associated with the early days of Glacier National Park, especially with the pre-Park period but also into the early years of the park. Schultz left his home in Boonville, New York, in 1877 and traveled to Blackfeet country east of what would later become Glacier National Park. Schultz was accepted into the company of the Blackfeet, and he lived with them and learned their culture and history over several years. He was given the Blackfeet name Apikuni (spellings vary). He married a Blackfeet woman, Nahtahki (sometimes spelled Natahki), in 1879, with whom a son was born in February 1882 (Hart Merriam Schultz, known primarily by his Blackfeet name Lone Wolf, who became a respected Blackfeet and western artist). Schultz lived with the Blackfeet until the passing of Nahtahki in 1903.[6, 7, 8]

In 1883, Schultz first visited the area later to become Glacier National Park, and he returned in 1884. He became quite familiar with the St. Mary and Swiftcurrent valleys there. In 1886, he and Nahtahki built a cabin and established a small ranch on the banks of the Two Medicine River east of the future Glacier Park. They lived there until Nahtahki's aforementioned passing. Schultz also began a business as a guide and outfitter for eastern visitors to the region. Schultz wrote and submitted an article on the Chief Mountain country on the northern edge of the future park and submitted it to the magazine *Forest and Stream* (the precursor to the more well-known *Field and Stream*). The editor of that magazine was none other than George Bird Grinnell, who as we saw in Chapters 1 and 2 of this book was hugely influential along with Louis Hill and the Great Northern Railway in getting Glacier declared a national park in 1910. Grinnell wrote Schultz and used his services as a guide for several trips to the area in the 1880s and 1890s. A noted author himself, Grinnell urged Schultz to put down on paper his knowledge of and experiences with the Blackfeet. After Nahtahki's passing in 1903, Schultz began to do so. The result, published as a book by *Forest and Stream* in 1907, was Schultz's first and now classic book, *My Life as an Indian.*[9, 10]

During the period following Nahtahki's passing, including the time he spent writing his classic book, Schultz moved away from Montana for his health. He did not return until 1914. Because of his fame as an author by that time, Schultz went to Louis Hill, president of the Great Northern Railway, with a proposition. In exchange for free lodging and transportation from the railroad and its subsidiary hotel company, Schultz would arrange a camping trip with his Blackfeet friends in Glacier National Park and produce a book about the camping trip and tales provided to him by his Blackfeet friends. Hill loved the idea and underwrote such an idea not only for the summer of 1915, but also for subsequent camping trips in 1922 and 1925. In the years between, Schultz made annual summer trips to the park with his travel and lodging underwritten by the railway. The 1915 trip, photographed both by himself and by Great Northern-employed photographer Roland Reed (Chapter 4), resulted in the publication (with ballyhooed Great Northern Railway sponsorship) of Schultz's well-known book *Blackfeet Tales of Glacier National Park*. The mining of tales from his Blackfeet friends in the summer of 1922 resulted in the book *Friends of My Life as an Indian* in 1923, and the 1925 camping trip with Blackfeet elders led to Schultz's book *Signposts of Adventure* published the following year.[11]

Right: Photo from James Willard Schultz's book *Blackfeet Tales of Glacier National Park* showing Schultz conversing with two Blackfeet chieftains on the shore of Two Medicine Lake. The photo was taken prior to publication of Schultz's book in 1916. (*R. Reed photo, from book in author's personal collection*)

Below: Titled "Opening of the Elk Medicine Pipe Ceremony," J. W. Schultz (at left) is shown with several members of the Blackfeet. Photo taken prior to 1916. (*R. Reed photo, from book in author's personal collection*)

Blackfeet camp on the shore of Upper Two Medicine Lake, *circa* 1920s. (*J.W. Schultz, photo; Montana State University*)

Mary Roberts Rinehart

Mary Roberts Rinehart was undoubtedly the most famous female writer to write about Glacier National Park and the Blackfeet, under the sponsorship of the Great Northern Railway. Primarily a mystery writer, Rinehart was often called the American Agatha Christie. Author of hundreds of works, most of which are forgotten today, she is remembered in Glacier National Park circles for her Great Northern-sponsored trips to the park in 1915 and 1916. In 1915, she joined the famous cowboy artist Charlie Russell on a multi-day horseback tour led by famous western wrangler Howard Eaton. This tour left from Glacier Park (East Glacier) and ended up eventually in Belton (West Glacier). In Glacier Park, Rinehart met with, and was appalled by the conditions of, the Blackfeet tribal members who greeted visitors to Glacier Park Station and Glacier Park Lodge. Deeply affected by her meetings with the Blackfeet, she became an advocate for their well-being in messages and visits to Congress. Her advocacy for the well-being of the Blackfeet resulted in her adoption by the tribe in May 1923, in a ceremony that gave her the honor of receiving the name Pitamakan (Pi-ta-mak-an), a revered name previously given only to a famous warrior woman of the tribe.[12, 13]

Author Mary Roberts Rinehart with four Blackfeet chiefs in Washington, D.C. Photo caption reads "Mary Roberts Rhinehart [*sic*], adopted member of the Blackfeet Indians snaped [*sic*] with four chiefs of the Tribe in Wash. D.C. today. Chief Mad Plume on her right, Chief Two Gun White Calf on her left. Miss Rhineharts [*sic*] Indian name is Pi-ta-mak-an, meaning running Eagle." (*Photographer uncredited, photo taken May 31, 1923. LOC 93508070*)

After her 1915 trip to Glacier Park, Rinehart wrote her classic book *Through Glacier Park: The Log of a Trip with Howard Eaton*. This book remains a classic in park literature to this day. On her 1916 trip, also sponsored by the Great Northern Railway, Rinehart traveled with her family, spending a brief time in the Glacier Park-Two Medicine area before traveling westward to Belton for a float trip down the North Fork of the Flathead River. This second (and last) trip to the park by Rinehart resulted in her subsequent book *Tenting To-night*.[14]

Although she never returned to Glacier National Park after her second trip in 1916, the publicity machine of the Great Northern Railway was not about to waste their investment in Rinehart's fame. They commissioned her to write an introduction to their travel booklet that touted both the park and the relationship between the park and the Blackfeet tribe. This introduction first appeared in 1918 and was used again in later editions fancifully titled *The Call of the Mountains* through at least the 1925 edition.[15, 16]

Mary Roberts Rinehart's two books on Glacier National Park, published in 1916 (left) and 1918 (right), both completed under the sponsorship of the Great Northern Railway. (*Both books from author's personal collection*)

Great Northern Railway brochure, *circa* 1918 (left), containing a photo of, and an introduction written by, Mary Roberts Rinehart (right). The right-hand photo shows Rinehart in the field in the Cataract Creek valley by Grinnell Lake below Grinnell Glacier. (*Both photos undated, left uncredited, right by Fred Kiser*)

6
GREAT NORTHERN-SUPPORTED ARTISTS SHOWCASING THE BLACKFEET

The Great Northern Railway promotional machine did not miss a beat. In addition to hiring photographers to take pictures (many for cheap, easily distributed postcards) of the Blackfeet in the new national park scenery, and writers to use words to forge the tie in the public mind between the park and the Blackfeet, the railway hired a variety of artists to design promotional materials that emphasized the link between Glacier National Park and the Blackfeet. These artists also produced more lasting artworks—paintings and sculptures—featuring "the Blackfeet Indians of Glacier National Park." The first such artist was the painter and illustrator Joe Scheuerle.

Joe Scheuerle

Joseph (Joe) Scheuerle grew up in Austria, where he was captivated by the American Wild West and Native Americans. After his family immigrated to the U.S. and settled in Cincinnati in 1882, Scheuerle eventually studied art at the Art Academy of Cincinnati, from which he graduated in 1896. He moved to Chicago in 1900 and was employed as a lithographer and illustrator. He drew posters for Wild West shows and portraits of Native Americans in those shows. In Chicago, he met Carolyn Lohrey, and they married in 1904. Joe made his first visit westward to visit and paint Native Americans in 1909, and in 1910 visited the new Glacier National Park and the Blackfeet Native Americans on the adjacent reservation. During this visit, he became acquainted with the president of the Great Northern Railway, Louis Hill, who was familiar with Joe's artistic renderings from the aforementioned Wild West shows. Hill hired Joe to create promotional materials for the new national park, including the railway's iconic mountain goat logo that encouraged viewers to "See America First." Hill also encouraged Scheuerle to create portraits of Blackfeet Native Americans that Hill could use in his campaign to associate in the public's mind the Blackfeet with Glacier National Park.[1, 2, 3]

Joe Scheuerle was painfully aware of the poverty and difficult conditions in which the reservation Blackfeet and other tribes lived. The portraits he painted often had notes written on the backside decrying the living conditions in which he found his subjects. He befriended his portrait subjects and allowed them the dignity of dressing themselves in whatever clothing they chose, rather than attempting to "portray them" in fanciful Native American regalia often not of their own tribe as other artists did. Although some of his promotional artwork of the Blackfeet for the Great Northern seems distasteful if not outright racist, it must be viewed through the lens of the period, and in the context of Scheuerle's respect and admiration for the Blackfeet people. The Blackfeet viewed him as a friend, and adopted him into the tribe in 1912, giving him the adopted name "Spotted Head."[4]

Artist Joe Scheuerle at home with a variety of Native American artifacts and memorabilia. (*Undated photo, unknown photographer; MHS p0002896*)

Above: Joe Scheuerle with three Native American men, probably Blackfeet. (*Undated photo, unknown photographer; MHS p0002907*)

Right: Joe Scheuerle with Native American man in traditional dress with lodge in background. (*Undated photo, unknown photographer; MHS p0002910*)

Above: Joe Scheuerle artwork for a Great Northern exhibit featuring Scheuerle's caricatures of tourists and Blackfeet people. (*Bain News Service photo, 1933; MHS p0002893*)

Left: Close-up view of Scheuerle's Blackfeet caricature art. Such politically incorrect material was common in the Great Northern's advertising campaign. The text of the sign reads "How! The robe is spread and the pipe is ready." (*Bain News Service, 1933; MHS p0002893*)

The annual Great Northern Railway calendar became an eagerly awaited yearly promotional release that featured portraits of Blackfeet Indians. Most people associate the annual calendar and Native American artwork with artist Winold Reiss (see below); however, the first artist utilized by the Great Northern for such a purpose was not Reiss, but rather Joe Scheuerle. The 1914 Great Northern calendar featured twelve portraits of Blackfeet Native Americans painted by Scheuerle. These portraits were also distributed as prints in a portfolio labeled "Blackfeet Indians of Glacier National Park." Like virtually all his artwork, Scheuerle held the copyright to each portrait. It was, perhaps, this insistence by Scheuerle that he held the copyrights to his work that led the Great Northern, in the 1920s, to move on to artist Winold Reiss for the monthly Blackfeet portraits in the railway's annual calendar.

A 1914 portfolio of Blackfeet portraits that had graced the 1914 Great Northern Railway monthly calendar, all the work of Joe Scheuerle. The colorized photo on the cover of the portfolio is the Fred Kaiser colorized photograph of Chief Two Guns White Calf. (*Photo by author, author's personal collection*)

Above left: Blackfeet scout White Grass, from the 1914 Joe Scheuerle portfolio of monthly Great Northern calendar portraits. (*Photo by author, author's personal collection*)

Above right: Blackfeet warrior Eagle Child, from the 1914 Joe Scheuerle portfolio of monthly Great Northern calendar portraits. (*Photo by author, author's personal collection*)

Left: Blackfeet Chief Wolf Plume, from the 1914 Joe Scheuerle portfolio of monthly Great Northern calendar portraits. (*Photo by author, author's personal collection*)

Above left: Blackfeet Chief Curly Bear, from the 1914 Joe Scheuerle portfolio of monthly Great Northern calendar portraits. (*Photo by author, author's personal collection*)

Above right: Blackfeet brave Wolf Eagle, from the 1914 Joe Scheuerle portfolio of monthly Great Northern calendar portraits. (*Photo by author, author's personal collection*)

Right: Blackfeet brave Buffalo Body, from the 1914 Joe Scheuerle portfolio of monthly Great Northern calendar portraits. (*Photo by author, author's personal collection*)

Winold Reiss

The artist probably most closely associated with the Great Northern Railway and the railway's desire to portray the Blackfeet people as "Glacier Park's Indians" was yet another Germanic artist, Winold Reiss. Born in Karlsruhe, Germany, in 1886, Reiss was fascinated with the American West like fellow Germanic artists Joe Scheuerle, Julius Seyler, and John Fery. Reiss immigrated to the United States in October 1913, where he settled in New York City.[5, 6, 7]

In 1919 (six years after arriving in New York), Reiss met a Blackfeet named Yellow Elk on an elevated train in Manhattan. Yellow Elk had worked as a circus rider and had been discharged when Reiss encountered him. Reiss employed him as a model, and from that relationship Reiss became determined to visit the ancestral home of the Blackfeet in northwest Montana.[8]

His appetite whetted by his encounter and work with Yellow Elk, Reiss departed for the Blackfeet Reservation in the early winter (perhaps unaware of the severity of Montana winters!) of 1920. Arriving via the Great Northern Railway in Browning, Reiss endeared himself to the Blackfeet he met with his open and respectful manner. He slowly earned their trust such that several of them began to agree to pose for him for portraits. Over a two-week period, he completed thirty-six portraits, many of which would be displayed later that spring in a New York gallery. The Blackfeet were impressed by the speed and energy with which Reiss painted, and towards the end of his visit they honored him with bestowing on him the Blackfeet name "Beaver Child" (Ksistakpoka) because of the speed with which he was able to paint their portraits. Many of the tribal elders painted during this visit by Reiss remained his friends and models for decades.[9, 10, 11]

Reiss would not return to Browning and Glacier National Park until 1927, but when he did it was under the sponsorship of Louis Hill and the Great Northern Railway. Reiss painted fifty-two portraits of Blackfeet during this trip, all of which were purchased by Hill. He returned again in 1928, producing more portraits purchased by Hill. These paintings allowed Hill to begin, in 1928, the issuance of the annual "Great Northern Blackfeet" calendar, a tradition that continued for decades. Hill also used the images on promotional posters, playing cards, and in magazine and newspaper advertisements. Lithographic prints of the portraits were sold in portfolios for collectors, and this portfolio also contained a booklet about the history of the Blackfeet written by western expert Frank Bird Linderman. Reiss' work with the Blackfeet became synonymous with Glacier National Park and the Great Northern Railway, and the labeling of Reiss' portfolio as "Blackfeet Indians of Glacier National Park" continued the branding tradition that had begun in the 1910s[12, 13, 14]

Reiss returned to Glacier Park in 1931, operating an independent art school on the park's east side. In 1933, he was appointed an assistant professor of mural painting at New York University. His ever-growing fame allowed him to convince the Great Northern Railway to partner with him and support his school. The railway's St. Mary Chalets were underutilized after the opening of Going-to-the-Sun Road in Glacier Park in 1933, and so the railway was happy to allow Reiss to use the chalets for his art school in the summers of 1934–1937. Reiss' brother Hans also taught there, hired by Winold Reiss to teach sculpting to complement Winold's painting lessons.[15, 16, 17, 18]

Winold once again returned to Glacier Park in 1943, during which time he completed

Above left: Artist Winold Reiss, 1934. (*Photo by W. T. Reiss, from Winoldreiss.org*)

Above right: Winold Reiss painting Buffalo Body, identified elsewhere as Medicine Boss Ribs, 1931. (*T. J. Hileman photo, umt010686*)

Winold Reiss, Aline Davis, and Bird Rattler at Reiss' Glacier Park summer art school, 1935. (*Photo by W. T. Reiss, from Winoldreiss.org*)

Above: Reiss portfolio of twenty-four prints of Blackfeet people, published by the Great Northern Railway in 1940. The portfolio also contained a short history of the Blackfeet written by Frank Bird Linderman. *(Author's personal collection)*

Left: Only Child, a young Blackfeet woman, painted by W. Reiss for his portfolio *Blackfeet Indians of Glacier National Park.* (*Author's personal collection*)

Above left: Two Guns (White Calf), painted by W. Reiss for his portfolio *Blackfeet Indians of Glacier National Park.* (*Author's personal collection*)

Above right: Lazy Boy, Blackfeet medicine man, painted by W. Reiss for his portfolio *Blackfeet Indians of Glacier National Park.* (*Author's personal collection*)

Above left: Night Shoots, a Blackfeet brave, painted by W. Reiss for his portfolio *Blackfeet Indians of Glacier National Park.* (*Author's personal collection*)

Above right: Scalping Woman, the wife of Night Shoots, painted by W. Reiss for his portfolio *Blackfeet Indians of Glacier National Park.* (*Author's personal collection*)

Undated photo of Winold Reiss' Glacier Park art school, showing students with Blackfeet models and Reiss at center with student. (*T. J. Hileman photo, umt013118*)

Artist and sculptor Hans Reiss, older brother of Winold Reiss, with a Blackfeet model and two students, probably at W. Reiss' Glacier Park summer art school. (*T. J. Hileman photo, undated; umt010687*)

an additional sixty-six portraits of Blackfeet tribal members. His last trip to the park was in 1948. Reiss died of a stroke on August 29, 1953. In July 1954, his ashes were taken to the Blackfeet tribal headquarters in Browning, where he was recalled as a good friend of the Blackfeet, one who respected them and their traditions, who made lasting friendships with many tribal members, and who paid fairly for the modeling provided by the Blackfeet. In a traditional Blackfeet ceremony on the eastern edge of Glacier Park, tribal elders scattered the ashes of Winold Reiss to the wind.[19]

Julius Seyler and John Fery

During the first several years of Glacier Park's existence, Great Northern Railway President Louis Hill engaged in a true frenzy of hiring artists to portray either or both the park's outstanding natural scenery, and the Blackfeet people who lived along the eastern edge of the park. We have already seen how Hill utilized the artistic skills of Joe Scheuerle to imprint in the public's mind the relationship between the Blackfeet and the new national park. Two additional Germanic artists, with strongly contrasting styles, were employed by Hill and the Great Northern in the 1910–1913 period. Julius Seyler (1873–1955), a striking late-Impressionist painter from Munich, Germany, was employed to portray the Blackfeet and the park-edge landscape in which they lived. John Fery (1859–1934), born in the Austrian Alps, was tasked by Hill from 1910–1913, and again in the mid-1920s, to produce vivid landscapes of the park's outstanding scenery, such that the resulting paintings could be displayed not only in Glacier Park Lodge and other Great Northern park facilities, but be sent to shows and galleries around the country to attract additional visitors to the railway's Glacier Park facilities. Interestingly, virtually none of Fery's landscape paintings included any Blackfeet people. Hill's instructions to Fery apparently told him to portray and emphasize only the outstanding natural landscape, whereas Julius Seyler was encouraged by Hill to portray the Blackfeet. This two-pronged approach was rather different than that utilized by the early park photographers hired by Hill and the Great Northern Railway (Kiser, Reed, and Hileman especially) whose photographs frequently illustrated Blackfeet people on the magnificent park landscape, albeit typically in posed, unrealistic situations. Although most of Fery's works were completed in a frenzy during the 1910–1913 period, Hill brought Fery back from 1925–1927 to portray the landscape around the new Prince of Wales Hotel in adjacent Waterton Lakes National Park, Alberta. This period was Fery's final commission from Hill and the railway.[20, 21, 22]

Julius Seyler, who was hired by Louis Hill and traveled with him to Glacier Park in 1913, worked primarily in the Many Glacier region in the summers of 1913 and 1914. He chose in his paintings to portray the Blackfeet not in their early twentieth-century poverty-stricken state, but rather as the proud people they had been in the still-remembered, recent historical past. His images of the Blackfeet are striking and powerful. He painted images of them on the landscape, but also did individual portraits of prominent tribal members, including Eagle Calf, Medicine Owl, Yellow Medicine, Two Guns White Calf, and Jack Big Moon.[23]

Seyler was a tall, athletic man whose paintings and work ethic appealed to the Blackfeet, such that Jack Big Moon personally adopted Seyler in July 1913. Big Moon named Seyler as Boss Ribs and bestowed upon him a protective spiritual charm that

Above: John Fery painting of Swiftcurrent Falls, *circa* 1913. (*BNSF Railway Foundation collection*)

Left: Artist Julius Seyler and Blackfeet Indian Jack Big Moon in Glacier National Park, 1914. (*Public domain photo, unattributed*)

Cover of W. Farr's biography of Julius Seyler that focused on Seyler's artistic work with the Blackfeet. (*Author's personal collection*)

Seyler subsequently wore wherever he traveled on the Blackfeet Reservation. This charm was his "go anywhere safely" pass to work with the Blackfeet and indicated to them Seyler's prominence as an adopted member of the tribe. Seyler became a good friend of Two Guns White Calf and his wife, Susan, and in 1914, Seyler displayed several of his paintings in the Glacier Park Hotel/Lodge in East Glacier with Two Guns and his wife at his side.[24]

Kathryn Leighton, Elsa Jemne, and Elizabeth Davey Lochrie

As we saw in Chapter 5, the Great Northern Railway was not averse to hiring women writers in their efforts to indelibly bond the Blackfeet with Glacier National Park in the public consciousness. Similarly, the railway hired several women artists to portray the "Glacier Park Blackfeet" in paintings that could be sent on traveling displays across the country. Three of the most prominent of these women artists were Kathryn Leighton, Elsa Jemna, and Elizabeth Davey Lochrie.

Kathryn Leighton was born in New Hampshire in 1875, studied art in Boston, and married in 1900. She and her husband moved to Los Angeles in 1910, and in her art studio there she painted hundreds of portraits of Native Americans, work that brought her international recognition. During a party in Los Angeles, Leighton was introduced to the cowboy artist Charlie Russell. Because of their shared interests in art and Native Americans, the two became good friends, and the Leightons began visiting Bull Head Lodge in Glacier National Park at Russell's invitation. Charlie Russell recommended that Kathryn Leighton contact officials of the Great Northern Railway as well as officials of the Blackfeet Nation in order to allow her to paint Blackfeet tribal members. In 1926, Leighton received a commission from the railroad to paint Blackfeet elders as part of the Great Northern's well-documented campaign to imprint in the public's mind the association between the Blackfeet and Glacier National Park. Leighton and her family were provided three months of free lodging in the park by the railroad, which also facilitated her meetings with Blackfeet whom she painted. The Blackfeet and the railroad were impressed by her paintings, so much so that the railroad paid high prices for twenty of the paintings, which were subsequently sent on a cross-country tour. The Blackfeet adopted Leighton into their tribe, giving her the name "Anna-Tar-Kee," meaning Beautiful Woman in Spirit. She passed away in 1952.[25, 26]

Elsa Jemne, born Elsa Laubach in St. Paul, Minnesota, in 1887, studied art in St. Paul and Philadelphia and won an award to study art in Europe. She married architect Magnus Jemne in 1917, and the couple settled in St. Paul. Jemne became well known for painting murals in public buildings in the upper Midwest, and in 1925 and 1926 was invited by Great Northern Railway President Ralph Budd to spend two months each summer painting portraits of the Blackfeet. She lived in a large teepee among the Blackfeet, and several of her portraits were painted in the tepee. Jemne also painted landscapes of Glacier Park while in the area. The Blackfeet appreciated Jemne's independence and willingness to live among them, and adopted her into their tribe in a ceremony in Fort Union, Montana. Jemne died in 1974, leaving a strong legacy of art associated with both Glacier National Park and especially the Blackfeet people.[27, 28]

Portrait of artist Kathryn Leighton, known for her distinctive portraits of Blackfeet tribal members. (*Vose Galleries, Boston, MA, photographer unattributed*)

Elsa Jemne painting Mrs. Curley Bear in Jemne's tepee, 1926. (*Photo by T. J. Hileman, MNHS N1.1 p146*)

Above left: Yellow Kidney, Keeper of the Beaver Bundle, a 1926 painting by Elsa Jemne. (*MHS Collection X1965.19.0*)

Above right: Elsa Jemne's adoption ceremony when she was adopted into the Blackfeet Tribe in Fort Union, MT. (*Photographer unknown, photo undated, MNHS por 11503 p2*)

Elizabeth Davey was born in July 1890 in Deer Lodge, Montana. She studied art at the Pratt Institute in Brooklyn, New York. She married local Montana banker Arthur J. Lochrie in 1913, and they were married for sixty-two years. In 1931, she made a trip to Glacier National Park, and subsequently returned annually to the park for many years. In the summers of 1933 and 1934, Lochrie studied with renowned park painter Winold Reiss, supported of course by the Great Northern Railway, at his school on the shore of St. Mary Lake. During her travels to Glacier Park, Lochrie became friends with Gypsy Bull Child, a Blackfeet woman she met in 1931 while sketching near the tepees of a Blackfeet encampment near the Many Glacier Hotel. Their friendship grew, and in the summer of 1932, Elizabeth returned to Glacier Park Station where she rented a cabin. The Bull Childs adopted her into their family and the Blackfeet, giving her the name "Net-chi-ta-ki," meaning Lone Woman, or Woman Who Came Alone. Her adoption allowed Lochrie to paint among the Blackfeet, and her portraits of them are highly prized. She learned the Blackfeet language and sign language, and she became a spokesperson and knowledgeable lecturer on behalf of their welfare. Lochrie continued to paint well into her eighties and passed away in 1981.[29, 30]

Photo of artist Elizabeth Davey Lochrie. (*Unknown date and photographer, Hockaday Museum of Art*)

Above: Hand-painted and handmade Christmas card by Elizabeth Lochrie, showing Blackfeet people and camp. (*Elizabeth Davey Lochrie Christmas card to W. Langdon Kihn, after 1931. W. Langdon Kihn papers, 1904–1990. Archives of American Art, Smithsonian Institution*)

Right: Heavy Breast—Blackfoot, oil on canvas painting by Elizabeth Lochrie, 1934. (*MHS 1979.12.105*)

John L. Clarke

John L. Clarke was born in Highwood, Montana (near Great Falls), on May 10, 1881. His mother was Blackfeet, and his father was Blackfeet and Scottish. Scarlet fever hit John at age two, rendering him deaf and unable to speak. Five of his brothers died from the disease. Because of his profound deafness and inability to speak, Clarke became known as Cutapuis, Blackfeet for "The Man Who Talks Not." His family moved to Midvale, later East Glacier Park, Montana, in 1888. John received his education at schools for the deaf in Montana and Wisconsin, where he learned drawing and sculpting. He especially excelled in woodcarving, for which as we shall see he became internationally famous and acclaimed.[31, 32]

After his schooling, Clarke returned to live in Midvale/East Glacier Park with his family, and where he established a studio. He would live in East Glacier for the rest of his life. In 1911, Clarke met Louis Hill of the Great Northern Railway during one of Hill's visits to East Glacier, and Clarke served as a guide for hikes along the eastern edge of Glacier National Park. Hill became acquainted with Clarke's carving abilities and eventually purchased numerous of Clarke's increasingly famous animal carvings for sale in the gift shops of the Great Northern's Glacier Park hotels. Hill also commissioned Clarke to carve wooden bears for the bases of the table lamps in Hill's Glacier Park hotels. Hill provided Clarke with a wood-carving shop in one of the chalets at Many Glacier and allowed Clarke to carve in the lobby of Glacier Park Lodge in East Glacier as an enticement for sales of his works and as a form of entertainment for the guests there.[33, 34]

Clarke's fame grew through showings of his works and awards won in locations including Philadelphia, Chicago, New York, Boston, London, and Paris. His works became highly prized by collectors, including (in addition to Louis Hill of the Great Northern) the cowboy artist Charlie Russell, John D. Rockefeller, and U.S. President Warren G. Harding. Clarke fast became known as "America's Wood Sculptor." A great deal of Clarke's fame and reputation rested squarely in the hands of Louis Hill (who claimed to have discovered Clarke) and his Great Northern's publicity machine, eager to tout the fame of one of "Glacier Park's Blackfeet." In addition to Hill providing Clarke with commissions and locations to carve for the benefit of the Great Northern's paying guests, Hill's publicity machine spun wild, largely untruthful stories to bolster Clarke's reputation. One such story was published in September 1913, which claimed that John L. Clarke had married Princess Dawn Mist, "best loved maid of the tribe"! As we have seen already, not only did the Blackfeet not have princesses, but Princess Dawn Mist herself was a completely fictional construct of the Great Northern Railway.[35, 36]

Clarke did, however, get married in 1918—not to Princess Dawn Mist, but to Marie Peters "Mamie" Simon. They met in 1916, when Clarke was carving and also serving as a trail guide along the eastern front of Glacier Park, and Mamie was working for a saddle horse ranch just outside of (somewhat) nearby Babb, Montana. Both Clarke and Mamie were in their late thirties when they married. Having become friends with Charlie Russell and his wife, also known as Mamie, who served as Russell's business manager, Mamie Clarke modeled herself after Mamie Russell and became John's publicity and business manager. Feeling themselves too old for children of their own, they eventually adopted a daughter, Joyce, who would turn John's East Glacier studio into a museum and monument to his memory after his passing in 1970.[37]

Above left: Sculptor John L. Clarke carving a bear in the lobby of Glacier Park Lodge in East Glacier. (*Bain News Service, circa 1915, LOC 2014693899*)

Above right: J. L. Clarke in his workshop *circa* 1920, carving. (*Bain News Service, LOC B2-6317-3*)

Right: J. L. Clarke with a dog in front of a cabin, likely his workshop in East Glacier Park, 1930. (*Photographer unknown, MHS p0012339*)

Above left: J. L. Clarke, holding a carved cow elk, with his adopted daughter Joyce, *circa* 1933. (*Photographer unknown, MHS p0006791*)

Above right: J. L. Clarke carving a bear in his chalet studio at Many Glacier, 1918. (*Photographer unknown, MHS p0003038*)

In order to take advantage of his two most well-known Blackfeet friends' fame, James Hill introduced John L. Clarke to Two Guns White Calf, the most famous of the widely travelled "Glacier Park's Blackfeet." Clarke was immensely impressed with Two Guns White Calf and produced two clay busts of him that were subsequently cast in bronze. Clarke considered Two Guns the most important visitor he ever had in his humble East Glacier art studio.[38]

7

BLACKFEET PUBLIC APPEARANCES AND PUBLICITY EXCURSIONS

We saw in Chapter 3 a variety of ways in which the Great Northern Railway exploited the Blackfeet in order to "brand together" Glacier National Park, and by extension the Great Northern, with the Blackfeet tribe. In this chapter, a closer look is provided at how this was done, in and adjacent to the park itself, and across the country on Great Northern-sponsored Blackfeet excursions.

Blackfeet Appearances in and around Glacier National Park

The Great Northern Railway's advertising efforts in the 1910s through at least the 1930s virtually guaranteed tourists that a visit to Glacier National Park, via the railroad of course, would result in encounters with members of the Blackfeet tribe. Even into the 1950s, tribal members were paid to greet visitors, both at Glacier Park Station and at the nearby Glacier Park Lodge. Ordinary visitors to the park would encounter Blackfeet as quickly as getting off the train at Glacier Park Station. There, tribal members were paid by the railway to make appearances timed to the eastbound and westbound arrival times of the railway's famous Empire Builder train. Visitors disembarking the train at Glacier Park Station were also greeted by tribal members on the extensive lawn leading from the train station up to the massive lodge. Tribal members would serve to greet visitors outside of, and inside, the massive Glacier Park Lodge where visitors invariably stayed during their first night. Tepees adorned the lawn of the lodge, often with tribal members mingling and answering questions. Tribal members would also greet the arrivals of the railroad-sponsored Glacier Park Transport Company's famous red "jammer" buses at the front entrance to Glacier Park Lodge.[1, 2]

Famous visitors were treated with even more extensive opportunities to interact with Blackfeet tribal members. Louis Hill insisted that he be kept informed about any famous visitor(s) coming to the park, and he would arrange for them to be treated as

V.I.P.s complete with interactions with the Blackfeet. Ceremonies were arranged by the railway to honor such distinguished guests, with presentations of gifts from the tribe (funded by the Great Northern Railway), and often with adoption ceremonies where the distinguished visitor(s) would be given a Blackfeet name and adopted into the tribe. Such ceremonies were dictated and funded by the railway, of course.[3]

A member of the Blackfeet tribe greets tourists at Glacier Park Station, 1912. (*Photographer unknown, Minnesota Historical Society*)

Opposite above: Blackfeet tribal member Fred Big Top poses with tourists in this hand-tinted glass slide illustrating the lobby of Glacier Park Lodge. (*B. L. Brown, photographer, circa 1913–1915; GLAC 3514*)

Opposite below: First Lady Helen Taft (arrow on photo) holding "the sacred wimpuss skin," *circa* 1910–1913, with Blackfeet tribal members and others in Glacier Park. (*Bain News Service photo, LOC 2014690748*)

"Miniature Indian tepee village" and Blackfeet on the front lawn of Glacier Park Lodge, *circa* 1915. (*Photographer unknown, umt013117*)

Curly Bear presenting a beaded gun case to General Hugh L. Scott on the lawn of Glacier Park Lodge, August 1925. (*Photographer unknown, LOC 93515481*)

Blackfeet men sitting on the lawn of Glacier Park Lodge, 1933. (*Photographer unknown, MHS p0009172*)

Blackfeet men and children greeters in front of Glacier Park Lodge, *circa* 1936–1938. (*Photographer unknown, MHS p0002806*)

Chief Bull, also known as Richard Sanderville, signed postcards for tourists at Glacier Park Lodge. His pictograph signature is shown on the side of his lodge. (*Undated and unattributed, circa 1930–1940; MHS p0002675*)

Five Blackfeet braves join a large crowd awaiting the arrival of President Franklin Roosevelt on the lawn of Glacier Park Lodge. The date is unspecified, but must be either August 1934 or October 1937, the dates of Roosevelt's only two visits to Glacier Park. Given the weather illustrated in the photograph, 1937 (October) seems unlikely. (*Photographer unknown, MHS p0009172*)

Four Blackfeet in tribal garb greet visitors at Glacier Park Lodge, *circa* 1940. (*T. J. Hileman photo; GNP HPF 1035*)

Photo display in Glacier Park Station depot, showing the 1937 Blackfeet adoption ceremony for actor Clark Gable on the front lawn of Glacier Park lodge. Man at center is identified as Theodore Last Star. (*Photo by author, taken July 2012, original photo by Great Northern Railway*)

Two Blackfeet greeters welcome visitors at Glacier Park Lodge, *circa* 1950s. (*Russell Bull photo; GLAC 11122*)

Blackfeet appearances were not, of course, restricted to Glacier Park Station and the adjacent Glacier Park Lodge. Blackfeet made appearances around the Many Glacier area and in the Two Medicine valley. They were particularly employed to attend special ceremonies in Glacier National Park. They participated in the ceremony for the dedication of the creating of the Waterton-Glacier International Peace Park, on June 18, 1932. In July 1933, the Blackfeet (as well as tribes from the west side of Glacier National Park) participated in the dedication of Going-to-the Sun Road that took place on July 15. And on August 5, 1934, the Blackfeet participated in the ceremony honoring President Franklin Roosevelt, his wife Eleanor, and Secretary of the Interior Harold Ickes during their visit to Glacier Park. The visit was to honor the efforts of the young men of the Civilian Conservation Corps across the western states, and to make one of Roosevelt's "fireside chat" radio broadcasts. The ceremony and radio broadcast took place on the shore of Two Medicine Lake at the Great Northern's Two Medicine Chalets. President Roosevelt, Mrs. Roosevelt, and Secretary Ickes were each adopted into the Blackfeet tribe and given tribal names.[4, 5]

Mrs. Bull, wife of Chief Bull, and Joe Butterfly pose for a Great Northern publicity photo, June 19, 1932. (*Photo unattributed; MHS p0002776*)

Joseph M. Dixon, center, is greeted by two unidentified Blackfeet women at the ceremony for the dedication of the creating of the Waterton-Glacier International Peace Park, June 18, 1932. (*Photo unattributed, umt010877*)

Tinted lantern slide showing Blackfeet tepees at Logan Pass for the July 15, 1933, dedication ceremonies for Going-to-the-Sun Road. (*George A. Grant photo, GLAC 5534*)

Blackfeet encampment at Logan Pass, although unspecified almost certainly during the dedication ceremony for Going-to-the-Sun Road (photo is dated July 15, 1933, the day of the dedication). (*Photographer unattributed, GNP HPF 4866*)

Five Blackfeet women in traditional dress, standing in front of a tepee at Logan Pass in Glacier Park on the dedication day for Going-to-the-Sun Road, July 15, 1933. (*Photographer unattributed, MHS p0002779*)

Blackfeet and Flathead Native Americans dance at the dedication ceremony for Going-to-the-Sun Road. (*G. A. Grant photo, July 15, 1933; GLAC 11426*)

Blackfeet Indians with famous American football coach Pop Warner (third from right) and his assistants at the Going-to-the-Sun Road dedication. (*G. A. Grant photo, July 15, 1933, GLAC 11453*)

Blackfeet tribal band at the Going-to-the-Sun Road dedication ceremonies at Logan Pass, July 15, 1933. (*G. A. Grant photo, GNP HPF 4981*)

Above: President Franklin D. Roosevelt and party listen to a presentation by Blackfeet elders on the shore of Two Medicine Lake in front of the main building of the Two Medicine Chalets, with Sinopah Mountain in the background across the lake. FDR, Eleanor Roosevelt (second from right), and Secretary of the Interior Harold Ickes were adopted into the Blackfeet tribe. (*Associated Press photo, August 5, 1934*)

Right: FDR and Secretary Ickes (right) after the president received a ceremonial headdress and peace pipe from the Blackfeet as part of their adoption into the tribe. (*Associated Press photo, August 5, 1934*)

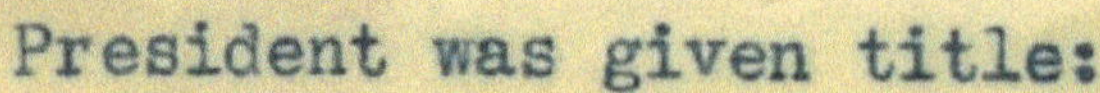

President was given title:

"Lone Chief"

Mrs. R. was named:

"Medicine Pipe Woman"
and
"Grand White Mother"

Sec. Ickes named:
"Big Bear"

File

Blackfeet Tribe

Blackfeet Agency
Browning, Montana
April 15, 1935

Honorable Franklin D. Roosevelt
President of the United States
The White House
Washington, D. C.

My dear President:

I have expressed you today the Certificate of your adoption into the Blackfeet Tribe of Indians last August, as I promised you.

You will note that the Certificate is framed by arrows but that there is no bow. This symbolizes the Blackfeet method of showing friendship and gratitude.

Wishing you every success in life, I am

Sincerely yours,

Richard Sanderville
Richard Sanderville. or
Chief Bull

Above: The honorary names given to President Roosevelt, Mrs. Roosevelt, and Secretary Ickes as certified in part of a letter from the Blackfeet tribe. (*FDR Library, Marist University PPF 2397*)

Left: Letter sent to President Roosevelt from Chief Bull (Richard Sanderville) of the Blackfeet the following spring, accompanying FDR's official Certificate of Adoption. (*FDR Library, Marist University PPF 2397*)

Blackfeet Excursions Outside Glacier National Park Sponsored by the Great Northern Railway

In Chapter 3 of this book, I alluded to the numerous wide-ranging publicity tours undertaken by groups of "Glacier Park's Indians" on behalf of the Great Northern Railway and described the visit to New York City in March 1913. No comprehensive list of such publicity tours is known to me, but here I present several photographic examples of the far-ranging efforts of the railway to use the Blackfeet to advocate for tourism to Glacier National Park and, by extension, for using the facilities there of the Great Northern Railway. In general, the farther the trip (such as to locations on the east or west coast), the more "whistle stops" that took place. Trips began soon after the creation of Glacier National Park in 1910, tailed off during World War I, and then increased again with the height of such excursions in the latter 1920s prior to the onset of the Great Depression. During these trips, a select group of "Glacier Park Indians" were paid to make public appearances as well as to meet other celebrities. Additionally, the Blackfeet typically provided entertainment in the form of war chants, tribal dances, and posing for photographs. Each member of the Blackfeet group was given business cards by Louis Hill, to be handed out to excursion visitors. These cards were designed to entice excursion visitors to come to Glacier National Park. On the left of the cards was a sketch of a Blackfeet tepee and the logo of the Great Northern Railway. Centered on the card was the individual Blackfeet's name, their job/position (including chief, medicine man, ranger, dancer, and so forth), and "Glacier National Park, Montana" for their address. The bottom of the card bore the inscription "Meet me at Glacier National Park next summer."[6, 7]

The Blackfeet publicity excursions sponsored by the Great Northern Railway ranged in length from several days up to two months. The list below, in chronological order, provides the general location and purpose of each excursion:

Carlisle, Pennsylvania, July 1912, Carlisle Indian School Commencement Week.
Chicago, Illinois, Minnesota–Chicago football game, and the Northwestern Land Products Show, unspecified date in November 1912.[8, 9]
Chicago, Illinois, present moccasins to opera singer Mary Garden, unspecified date, 1913.
New York City, New York, McAlpin Hotel at the national Travel and Vacation Show, March 1913.
Portland, Oregon, Rose Festival, June 1913.[10]
Washington, D.C., National Archives for language translation, February 1916.
New York City, New York, Commodore Hotel (visit reason unspecified), May 1921.[11, 12]
Chicago, Illinois, meeting with Chicago mayor, June 2, 1921.[13]
Spokane, Washington, National Indian Congress, October 1925.
Washington, D.C., meeting with President Calvin Coolidge, September 17, 1927.
Cleveland, Ohio, meeting with City Manager Hopkins, September 18, 1927.
Baltimore, Maryland, Baltimore and Ohio Railroad's Fair of the Iron Horse, September 24 to October 8, 1927.
Philadelphia, Pennsylvania, public appearance on return from Baltimore Fair, October 21, 1927.[14]
New York City, New York, meeting with mayor Jimmy Walker, October 1927.

Oxford, Ohio, received keys to the city on return trip from Baltimore Fair of the Iron Horse, October 1927.
Indianapolis, Indiana, various functions including meeting with Indiana governor, October 31, 1927.[15, 16]
Stockton, California, visit to College of the Pacific, July 31, 1928.
Lawrence, Kansas, attended dedication of Haskell Stadium at Haskell Indian College (now Haskell Indian Nations University), October 27, 1930.

"Mary Garden and Indians from Glacier Park." In 1913, a contingent of Blackfeet chiefs traveled via the Great Northern Railway to Chicago, to present a pair of handmade moccasins to the Indian maid Natomah, an opera role played by operatic star Mary Garden. *Natomah* is an opera in three acts by Victor Herbert. (*Unknown photographer from "The Outlook Magazine", 1913*)

Opposite above: Colorized photo of Blackfeet chief Mountain Chief interpreting a recording with ethnologist Frances Densmore in Washington, D.C., February 9, 1916. (*Harris and Ewing photo, LOC 200466775*)

Opposite below: Blackfeet tribal members and lodges in Spokane, WA, at the 1925 Spokane National Indian Congress. (*Photographer unattributed, MHS p0009675*)

WINSHIP & SONS
BLACKFEET INDIANS
GLACIER NAT'L PARK

A Blackfeet chief blessing a new Great Northern Railway engine at Glacier Park Station, technically outside the park, in 1927. Photo is on display in the depot at Glacier Park Station. (*Photo by author of a Great Northern Railway photo; MHS p0009675*)

Above: President Calvin Coolidge (center) with Commissioner of Indian Affairs Burke and several Blackfeet tribal members including Owen Heavy Breast (far left) and "Princess Dawn Mist" (here played by Irene Goss) in front of the White House, September 17, 1927. (*Underwood and Underwood photo; LOC 96519601*)

Right: Captioned "Princess Dawn Mist decorates City Manager Hopkins," on the reverse was noted "W.R. Hopkins becomes a brave." Irene Goss also played Princess Dawn Mist here. Photo taken September 18, 1927. (*Cleveland Press Collection, Michael Schwartz Library, Cleveland State University*)

8
CHIEF TWO GUNS WHITE CALF

Two Guns White Calf, also known as John Two Guns White Calf or John Two Guns, was one of the most well-known Native Americans of any tribe in the first half of the twentieth century (I will refer to him simply as "Two Guns" from here on in this chapter's text). He was born on the Blackfeet Reservation near Fort Benton in 1871 and was the adopted son of Chief White Calf and Hands Together. Two Guns died on March 12, 1934. His cause of death, listed on his official Death Certificate, was pulmonary tuberculosis, although some sources suggest he died of flu or due to complications from a broken leg sustained in a fall from a horse. His occupation was listed as "Rancher." His passing was noted in newspaper obituaries across the country, most notably including *The New York Times*. Nearly all these obituaries noted that he was the "Buffalo/Indian Head Nickel" model. The truth of such a claim is discussed below. Two Guns is buried in the Catholic cemetery in the Blackfeet tribal headquarters town of Browning, Montana.[1, 2, 3, 4]

Two Guns was good friends with both James J. Hill, founder of the Great Northern Railway, and his son Louis W. Hill (known for his widespread promotional efforts; see Chapters 2 and 3), and was a frequent visitor to Louis Hill's home in St. Paul, Minnesota. Two Guns traveled widely for the Great Northern for over twenty years and allowed his image to be used in a diversity of advertising forms (including pamphlets, desk blotters, magazine ads, and images painted by Great Northern-sponsored painters). In the process of these travels as well as his acting as a greeter and tribal spokesman at Glacier Park Station, Glacier Park Lodge, and in Washinton, D.C. Two Guns presented a dignified image and worked for Blackfeet rights, pressing Congress and the Bureau of Indian Affairs to provide promised funding for the tribe. Two Guns was widely photographed around the country and with prominent individuals of the period. These travels and publicity opportunities would have, in and of themselves, made Two Guns one of the best-known Native Americans in the United States. But what really sealed the deal was the simple five-cent piece known as the Buffalo or Indian-Head Nickel.[5, 6, 7]

Right: A 1929 press photo of silent screen actress Dorothy Janis, noted on the rear of the photo as being of one-eighth Cherokee heritage, and Two Guns White Calf. (*Photographer unattributed, photo by Underwood and Underwood*)

Below: "Supt. Friedman and Blackfeet Indians, Commencement Week, Carlisle, PA." Two Guns White Calf is labelled by the number 4 and has his hands on the shoulders of the superintendent. (*Photo taken July 23, 1912, photographer unattributed, public domain photo*)

New York City Mayor Jimmy Walker on the steps of City Hall with representatives of the Blackfeet. The mayor is flanked by Two Guns White Calf (left) and Owen Heavy Breast (right). "Princess Dawn Mist" is next to Heavy Breast. Note once again the buffalo nickel medallion worn by White Calf. (*Times World Wide Photos, October 23, 1927*)

Postcard caption reads: "The William Crooks train, first to operate in the northwest in 1861, on what is now a part of the Great Northern Railway, and the Blackfeet Indians of Glacier National Park and Waterton Lakes National Park, in attendance at the Baltimore and Ohio Railroad's Fair of the Iron Horse." Two Guns White Calf is in the upper row, third from left beneath the smokestack. (*Great Northern Railway photo, public domain photo, 1927*)

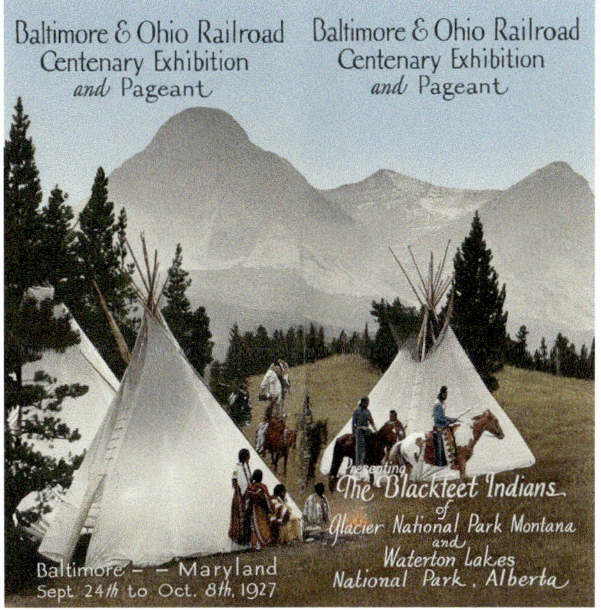

Right: Pamphlet advertising the 1927 Baltimore and Ohio Railroad Exhibition and Pageant, at which approximately thirty Blackfeet tribal members appeared, having ridden from Glacier Park Station to Baltimore on the Great Northern Railway on a train pulled by the original William Crooks engine. (*Baltimore and Ohio Railroad*)

Below: Charles W. Galloway, vice president of the Baltimore and Ohio Railroad Company, being adopted into the Blackfeet tribe during the B&O Exhibition and Pageant, 1927. Two Guns White Calf stands in the photo to the left of the man holding the drum. (*Photographer unidentified; LOC 2002723695*)

Baltimore and Ohio Railroad Company civil engineer Olive Dennis, with Bird Rattler and Two Guns White Calf at the 1927 B&O Exhibition and Pageant. Note Two Guns White Calf's usual Shriner's and buffalo nickel medallions. (*Photographer unattributed, public domain photo*)

Famous football coach Amos Alonzo Stagg (center right, holding hat) with students of the College of the Pacific, and Blackfeet guests, July 31, 1928. Two Guns White Calf stands next to Stagg (on left in photo), with Owen Heavy Breast at far right in front row. (*Photographer unknown, public domain photo*)

Above: Blackfeet delegation at the dedication of the football stadium of the Haskell Institute (today, Haskell Indian Nations University), Lawrence, Kansas, October 27, 1930. Two Guns White Calf stands at far left. (*Photographer unknown, public domain photo*)

Right: Two Guns White Calf (right) with another Blackfeet tribal member (who wears an actual upright Blackfeet war bonnet) and author Mary Roberts Rinehart, July 30, 1918. Location unspecified, but likely Glacier Park Station. (*Photographer unknown, public domain photo*)

Two Guns White Calf in what appears to be a men's clothing store/haberdashery, July 16, 1925. The location is unspecified. (*Photographer unknown, public domain photo*)

Two Guns White Calf with Montana Governor John E. Erickson, *circa* 1925–1933. Location is unspecified, possibly Glacier Park Station (East Glacier Park). (*Bain News Service, LOC 2014718526*)

An invitation from

CHIEF TWO GUNS WHITE CALF

of **Glacier National Park**

O-ki *(Greetings)* The Blackfeet Indians bid you welcome to our mountain homeland in Glacier National Park. Where once our buffalo-skin tepees were, today, in settings of rare scenic beauty, are great modern hotels and comfortable chalets affording hospitality for thousands. Here you may hike, ride horseback, motor, cruise mountain lakes, fish ice-fed trout streams, or loaf as you please.

Broad automobile highways lead from the "Big Trees Lodge" on the Great Northern Railway to many of the beauty spots, while others are comfortably reached afoot or on horseback over well-made trails. And the palatial Prince of Wales Hotel, just across the boundary in Waterton Lakes National Park, Canada, enables you to enjoy the Alpine grandeur of two nations in one memorable visit. Write to me for booklets regarding this great American scenic region. Mail the coupon today.

(Signed)
TWO-GUNS-WHITE-CALF
(His Mark)

GREAT NORTHERN

ROUTE OF THE NEW ORIENTAL LIMITED

A dependable railway

CHIEF TWO-GUNS-WHITE-CALF N. G.-2
c/o GREAT NORTHERN RAILWAY, Glacier Park, Montana
Please send me the free books about Glacier National Park. I am particularly interested in:
☐ General Tour of the Park ☐ Burlington Escorted Tour
*Name*________ *Address*________

A 1928 Great Northern print ad featuring Two Guns White Calf inviting visitors to come to Glacier and Waterton Lakes National Parks. (*Great Northern Railway*)

Two Guns White Calf and Owen Heavy Breast receiving the keys to the city of Oxford, Ohio, 1927. Note the medallions on Two Guns' chest. (*Frank R. Snyder photo, public domain*)

Adoption ceremony of Floyd Hockenhull, Kansas journalist and tour manager, into the Blackfeet tribe, June 26, 1928. Owen Heavy Breast at left, Two Guns White Calf at right. Blackfeet children and other man are unidentified. (*Photo by James Hockenhull, donated to Blackfoot Digital Library, Lethbridge, Alberta*)

Two Guns White Calf meets middleweight boxer Mike Gibbons, the "St. Paul Phantom," July 31, 1929, at an unspecified location. (*Bain News Service, LOC 2014716146*)

Two Guns White Calf and German diplomat Adolf Georg Otto "Ago" von Maltzan compare pipes, August 2, 1929. Location of the photo is unspecified. (*Bain News Service, LOC 2014704774*)

As we have seen, the Great Northern Railway's publicity machine never felt bound by the truth. When the Buffalo/Indian Head Nickel was released, Louis Hill encouraged the spreading of a story that Two Guns was the model for the nickel, thus further enhancing in the public's mind the linkage between the Great Northern Railway and the Blackfeet tribe, and by extension the linkage between the tribe and Glacier National Park (and all the tourism money that such linkages would accrue). As shown in several photos in this chapter, Two Guns himself took to wearing an oversized medallion illustrating the front of the nickel and claiming that he was indeed the model for the nickel. And as noted, upon Two Gun's death, obituaries across the country noted that he had been the model for the nickel.[8, 9]

So why was it so difficult to prove or disprove that Two Guns was the model for the coin? It apparently had to do with some of Two Guns' political leanings, which were seen at odds with the gentle, helpful image of him as a spokesperson for the Blackfeet as put forward by the Great Northern. The Kansas City Public Library explained it in the following way:

> A widely held belief, by some historians, is that Chief Two Guns was the main model for the Indian Nickel. The Chief headed a secret group known as the "Mad Dog Society" whose purpose was to protect and sustain the Blackfoot Heritage. Chief Two Guns was very outspoken about US policies and the mistreatment of Native Americans. The Government, at the time, feared that Chief Two Guns might incite the Blackfoot warriors to a confrontation in order [to] regain their lands, thus painting the Chief in a not so favorable light. The story was spread by US Officials that his image was not on the coin, attributing the likeness to a composite of three Native Americans: Two Moons, Big Tree and Iron Trail.[10]

And as of this writing in the year 2025, the controversy as to whose image is on the nickel remains, regardless of what was put forward by the Great Northern Railway. But Two Guns' legacy as a statesman working for the Blackfeet and Native American rights will endure.

Above left: Photograph of Two Guns White Calf, July 11, 1929. He wears two large medallions. The upper is a Shriner's Medallion, and the lower is a replica of the front of the Buffalo Nickel, showing the Native American face in profile that numerous news stories of the period stated was his profile. (*Photographer unknown, public domain photo*)

Above right: Undated profile photo of Two Guns White Calf. (*T. J. Hileman photo for Great Northern Railway*)

Front profile of the Buffalo/Indian Head nickel. Compare this to the previous photo of the profile of Two Guns White Calf. (*Public domain photo*)

AFTERWORD

THE GREAT NORTHERN RAILWAY AND "GLACIER PARK'S BLACKFEET"

The Great Northern Railway, in order to boost tourism to the new Glacier National Park created in 1910, embarked on a frankly ruthless campaign to indelibly link the Blackfeet tribe with the new national park in the public mind. Done for the purpose of making money from its investments in the railroad and the hotel and chalet infrastructure it had built in the 1910s, some tribal members clearly benefitted from this relationship, although the tribe had no say whatsoever in whatever decisions that were made by the Great Northern. Railway president Louis Hill was friends with several Blackfeet, especially those who traveled around the country in order to advertise and advocate for visiting Glacier Park. He provided some of them with gifts in the form of food and clothing, but needing to do so spoke volumes about the impoverished conditions on the reservation in the early twentieth century. And for the perhaps dozens of Blackfeet who benefitted from Hill's largesse, thousands of others across the reservation continued to suffer from poverty, unemployment, disease, and loss of their traditional way of life. Those conditions were not primarily caused by the Great Northern Railway, but rather by U.S. Government policies. But the Great Northern Railway worked in concert with the government to have Glacier National Park created in 1910 and cheerfully exploited the geographic proximity of the Blackfeet people to the new park for the railway's economic benefit. At the end of the day, as the saying goes, it was all about the money.

ENDNOTES

Introduction

1 The Blackfoot Gallery Committee, *The Story of the Blackfoot People: Niitsitapiisinni* (Buffalo, NY: Firefly Books, 2013), pp. 10-12.
2 Ewers, J. C., *The Story of the Blackfeet* (Lawrence, KS: U.S. Department of the Interior, Branch of Education, Bureau of Indian Affairs, 1944), p. 7.
3 Hall, R., *Beneath the Backbone of the World: Blackfoot People and the North American Borderlands, 1720–1877* (Chapel Hill, NC: University of North Carolina Press, 2020), p. 3.
4 Thompson, S., Kootenai Culture Committee, and Pikunni Traditional Association, *People Before the Park: The Kootenai and Blackfeet Before Glacier National Park* (Helena, MT: Montana Historical Society Press, 2015), p. 11.
5 Scriver, B., *The Blackfeet: Artists of the Northern Plains: the Scriver Collection of Blackfeet Indian Artifacts and Related Objects, 1894–1990* (Kansas City, MO: The Lowell Press, Inc., 1990), various pages.
6 Taliaferro, J., *Grinnell: America's Environmental Pioneer and His Restless Drive to Save the West* (New York City, NY: Liveright Publishing Corporation, 2019), p. xv.
7 *Ibid.*, pp. xv-xvi.
8 Hall, *op. cit.*, p. 9.

Chapter 1

1 Farr, W. E., *The Reservation Blackfeet, 1882–1945: A Photographic History of Cultural Survival* (Seattle, WA: University of Washington Press, 1984, paperback ed. 1986), various pages.
2 Taliaferro, J., *Grinnell: America's Environmental Pioneer and His Restless Drive to Save the West* (New York City, NY: Liveright Publishing Corporation, 2019), pp. 211-227.
3 Butler, D. R., *Cowboy Artist Charlie Russell and Glacier National Park* (Charleston, SC: Fonthill Media, 2024), various pages.
4 Wood, C. R., *Lines West: Great Northern* (Burbank, CA: Superior Publishing Company, 1967), various pages.
5 Taliaferro, *op. cit.*, p. 272.

6 *Ibid.*, various pages.
7 *Ibid.*, p. 290.
8 Peterson, L. L., *Edward S. Curtis: Printing the Legends—Looking at Shadows in a West Lit Only by Fire* (Helena, MT: Sweetgrass Books, 2024), pp. 64-68.
9 Grafe, S. L. (ed.), *Lanterns on the Prairie: The Blackfeet Photographs of Walter McClintock* (Norman, OK: University of Oklahoma Press, 2009), p. 53.
10 *Ibid.*, pp. 55-67.
11 McClintock, W., *The Old North Trail: Life, Legends and Religion of the Blackfeet Indians* (Lincoln, NE: University of Nebraska Press, 1968 edition reproduced from the 1920 first edition), various pages.

Chapter 2

1 Diettert, G. A., *Grinnell's Glacier: George Bird Grinnell and the Founding of Glacier National Park* (Missoula, MT: Mountain Press Publishing Company, 1992), p. 94.
2 Young, B. W., and McCormack, E. R., *The Dutiful Son: Louis W. Hill—Life in the Shadow of the Empire Builder* (St. Paul, MN: Ramsey County Historical Society, 2010), pp. 110-111.
3 Taliaferro, J., *Grinnell: America's Environmental Pioneer and His Restless Drive to Save the West* (New York City, NY: Liveright Publishing Corporation, 2019), p. 366.
4 Peterson, L. L., "The Call of the Mountains: Louis Hill and Glacier National Park," *Russell's West, The C.M. Russell Museum Magazine* (Great Falls, MT: C.M. Russell Museum, 2002), pp. 3-4.
5 Young and McCormack, *op. cit.*, p. 116.
6 Jones, D. W., *The Great Northern Railway in Marias Pass* (Charleston, SC: Arcadia Publishing, 2017), p. 32.
7 Moylan, B., *Glacier's Grandest: A Pictorial History of the Hotels and Chalets of Glacier National Park* (Missoula, MT: Pictorial Histories Publishing Company, Inc., 1995), various pages.
8 Djuff, R., and Morrison, C., *Glacier's Historic Hotels and Chalets: View with a Room* (Helena, MT: Farcountry Press, 2001), various pages.
9 Guthrie, C. W., *All Aboard! For Glacier: The Great Northern Railway and Glacier National Park* (Helena, MT: Farcountry Press, 2004), various pages.
10 Djuff and Morrison, *op. cit.*, various pages.

Chapter 3

1 Young, B. W., and McCormack, E. R., *The Dutiful Son: Louis W. Hill—Life in the Shadow of the Empire Builder* (St. Paul, MN: Ramsey County Historical Society, 2010), pp. 121-128.
2 *Ibid.*, various pages.
3 *Ibid.*, p. 122.
4 Great Northern Railway, *Blackfeet Indians of Glacier National Park* (St. Paul, MN: Great Northern Railway, 1914), various pages.
5 Great Northern Railway, *Glacier National Park* (St. Paul, MN: Great Northern Railway, undated, *circa* 1918), various pages.
6 Great Northern Railway, *The Call of the Mountains: Vacations in Glacier National* Park (St. Paul, MN: Great Northern Railway, 1925), various pages.
7 Wyckoff, W., and Dilsaver, L. M., "Promotional Imagery of Glacier National Park," *The Geographical Review*, Vol. 87 No. 1 (New York, NY: American Geographical Society, 1997), various pages.

8 Glacier Park Foundation, *A Historical Handbook for the Employees of Glacier Park Lodge* (St. Paul, MN: Glacier Park Foundation, 2016), various pages.
9 Glacier Park Hotel Company, *Picture Writing by the Blackfeet Indians in Glacier Park Hotels* (Glacier Park, MT: Glacier Park Hotel Company, *circa* 1915), entire document.
10 Butler, D. R., *Pioneering Women of Glacier National Park* (Charleston, SC: Fonthill Media, 2023), pp. 18-22.
11 Cahill, C. D., "The Indian Princess Who Wasn't There: The Strange Case of Dawn Mist," Chapter 5 in *Recasting the Vote: How Women of Color Transformed the Suffrage Movement* (Chapel Hill, NC: The University of North Carolina Press, 2020), pp. 72-75.
12 Schutz, L., "The Blackfoot Indians in New York City: Historic Photos from the Museum of the City of New York," *HuffPost* (www.huffpost.com/entry/the-blackfoot-indians-in_b_847936, 2011).

Chapter 4

1 Butler, D. R., *Early Photographers of Glacier National Park* (Charleston, SC: America Through Time, 2022), p. 36.
2 *Ibid.*, p. 36
3 Jones, D., *Glacier National Park: The Great Northern Railway Fred Kiser Artographs 1909–1912* (Liberty Lake, WA: Montana Railroads, 2021), p. 14.
4 *Ibid.*, p. 14.
5 *Ibid.*, various pages.
6 Butler, *op. cit.*, pp. 39-45.
7 *Ibid.*, pp. 51-56.
8 *Ibid.*, pp. 51-56.
9 Ruby, J., "Photographs of the Piegan by Roland Reed (Photo Essay)," *Studies in Visual Communication*, Vol. 7 No. 1 (Philadelphia, PA: University of Pennsylvania, 1981), various pages
10 Lawrence, E. R., *Alone with the Past: The Life and Photographic Art of Roland W. Reed* (Afton, MN: Afton Press, 2012), p. 15.
11 Butler, *op. cit.*, pp. 46-50.
12 *Ibid.*, pp. 57-63.

Chapter 5

1 Butler, D. R., *Pioneering Women of Glacier National Park* (Charleston, SC: Fonthill Media, 2023), pp. 67-71.
2 Flandrau, G., *The Story of Marias Pass* (St. Paul, MN: Great Northern Railway, 1925).
3 Laut, A. C., *The Blazed Trail of the Old Frontier* (New York, NY: Robert M. McBride & Company, 1926).
4 Laut, A. C., *Enchanted Trails of Glacier Park* (New York, NY: Robert M. McBride & Company, 1926).
5 Thompson, M., *High Trails of Glacier National Park* (Caldwell, ID: The Caxton Printers, Ltd., 1936).
6 Jermunson, D., *Blackfeet and Glacier Park: The Rest of the Story* (Kalispell, MT: Insty-Prints, 2009), pp. 1-3.
7 Montana Historical Society, *Blackfeet Man: James Willard Schultz* (Helena, MT: Montana Historical Society, 1961), pp. 1-3.
8 Hanna, W. L., *Stars Over Montana: Men Who Made Glacier National Park History* (West Glacier, MT: Glacier Natural History Association, 1988), pp. 96-100.
9 *Ibid.*, pp. 101-104.

10 Schultz, J. W., *My Life as an Indian* (Greenwich, CT: Fawcett Publications, Inc., reprint of book published by Forest and Stream Magazine, 1907), entire volume.
11 Hanna, *op. cit.*, pp. 105-106.
12 Butler, D. R., *Cowboy Artist Charlie Russell and Glacier National Park* (Charleston, SC: Fonthill Media, 2024), pp. 41-59.
13 Butler, *op. cit.* 2023, pp. 61-66.
14 Rinehart, M. R., *Tenting To-night: A Chronical of Sport and Adventure in Glacier Park and the Cascade Mountains* (Boston, MA: Houghton Mifflin Company, 1918), various pages.
15 Great Northern Railway, *Glacier National Park* (St. Paul, MN: Great Northern Railway, undated, *circa* 1918), interior unpaginated.
16 Great Northern Railway, *The Call of the Mountains: Vacations in Glacier National* Park (St. Paul, MN: Great Northern Railway, 1925), interior unpaginated.

Chapter 6

1 Boileau, T. I., and Boileau, M., "Joe Scheuerle: Modest Man with Friendly Palette," *Montana, The Magazine of Western History*, Vol. 21 No. 4 (Helena, MT: Montana Historical Society, 1971), p. 56.
2 Bottomly-O'looney, J., "Sitting Proud: The Indian Portraits of Joseph Scheuerle," *Montana, The Magazine of Western History*, Vol. 58 No. 3 (Helena, MT: Montana Historical Society, 2008), pp. 66-68.
3 Butler, D. R., *Cowboy Artist Charlie Russell and Glacier National Park* (Charleston, SC: Fonthill Media, 2024), pp. 33-37.
4 Boileau and Boileau, *op. cit.*, p. 56.
5 Raczka, P., *Winold Reiss Portraits of the Races* (Great Falls, MT: C.M. Russell Museum, 1986), p. 7.
6 WinoldReiss.org, "Winold Reiss Chronology" (WinoldReiss.org., 2014), winoldreiss.org/life/chronology.htm.
7 Kushner, M. S., *The Art of Winold Reiss: An Immigrant Modernist* (New York City, NY: New York Historical Society Museum and Library, 2021), pp. 11, 22.
8 Raczka, *op. cit.*, pp. 8-9.
9 *Ibid.*, pp. 10-18.
10 WinoldReiss.org, "Winold Reiss Chronology" (WinoldReiss.org., 2014), winoldreiss.org/life/chronology.htm.
11 Museum of the Plains Indian, *Connections: The Blackfeet and Winold Reiss* (Browning, MT: Museum of the Plains Indian, iacbmuseums-viewingroom.exhibit-e.art/viewing-room/connections-the-blackfeet-and-winold-reiss#tab:slideshow;tab-1:thumbnails, undated).
12 WinoldReiss.org, *op. cit.*
13 Museum of the Plains Indians, *op. cit.*
14 Linderman, F. B., *Out of the North: A Brief Historical Sketch of the Blackfeet Indian Tribe* (St. Paul, MN: Great Northern Railway Co., 1935), complete document.
15 WinoldReiss.org., *op. cit.*
16 Museum of the Plains Indians, *op. cit.*
17 Kushner, *op. cit.*, p. 91.
18 Raczka, *op. cit.*, pp. 35-41.
19 *Ibid.*, p. 50.
20 Farr, W. E., *Julius Seyler and the Blackfeet: An Impressionist at Glacier National Park* (Norman, OK: University of Oklahoma Press, 2009), various pages.
21 Peterson, L. L., *John Fery: Artist of Glacier National Park & the American West* (Hayden, ID: The Coeur d' Alene Art Auction, 2015), various pages.

22 *Ibid.*, various pages.
23 *Ibid.*, p. 139.
24 Farr, *op. cit.*, pp. 91-96, 154, 188.
25 Ivy, T., Gillenwater, E., Kellogg, D., and Moss, E., *A Timeless Legacy: Women Artists of Glacier National Park* (Kalispell, MT: Hockaday Museum of Art, 2015), pp. 19-22.
26 Butler, D. R., *Pioneering Women of Glacier National Park* (Charleston, SC: Fonthill Media, 2023), pp. 91-92.
27 Ivy *et al.*, *op. cit.*, pp. 23-25.
28 Butler, *op. cit.*, pp. 94-96.
29 Ivy *et al.*, *op. cit.*, pp. 27-30.
30 Butler, *op. cit.*, pp. 97-99.
31 Peterson, L. L., *The Call of the Mountains: The Artists of Glacier National Park* (Tucson, AZ: Settlers West Galleries, 2002), p. 137.
32 Peterson, L. L., *Blackfeet John L. "Cutapuis" Clarke and The Silent Call of Glacier National Park* (Helena, MT: Montana Historical Society, 2019), various pages.
33 Peterson, 2002, *op. cit.*, p. 138.
34 Peterson, 2019, *op. cit.*, various pages.
35 Peterson, 2002, *op. cit.*, pp. 138-139.
36 Peterson, 2019, *op. cit.*, pp. 136-137.
37 *Ibid.*, pp. 141-143.
38 *Ibid.*, pp. 204-207.

Chapter 7

1 Guthrie, C. W., *All Aboard! For Glacier: The Great Northern Railway and Glacier National Park* (Helena, MT: Farcountry Press, 2004), pp. 73-74.
2 Djuff, R., and Morrison, C., *Glacier's Historic Hotels and Chalets: View with a Room* (Helena, MT: Farcountry Press, 2001), pp. 32-34.
3 *Ibid.*, p. 35.
4 *Ibid.*, p. 39
5 Butler, D. R., *The Civilian Conservation Corps in Glacier National Park, Montana* (Charleston, SC: America Through Time, 2022), pp. 112-121.
6 Young, B. W., and McCormack, E. R., *The Dutiful Son: Louis W. Hill—Life in the Shadow of the Empire Builder* (St. Paul, MN: Ramsey County Historical Society, 2010), p. 9.
7 Peterson, L. L., *Blackfeet John L. "Cutapuis" Clarke and The Silent Call of Glacier National Park* (Helena, MT: Montana Historical Society, 2019), p. 116.
8 Young and McCormack, *op. cit.*, p. 8-9.
9 Associated Press, "Indian Guests in Hill Box Party," *Chicago Inter-Ocean* (Chicago, IL: Associated Press, November 1912), page and day unspecified.
10 Peterson, *op. cit.*, p. 115.
11 New York Evening World, "Classic-Faced Two Guns White Calf, Immortalized on the American Nickel, Balks at a Tepee on N.Y. Skyscraper," *New York Evening World*, New York, NY, May 2, 1921, p. 3.
12 New York Herald Sun, "Real Indians from the Mountains Looking Over New York's Towering Pinnacles from the Roof of the Hotel Commodore," *New York Herald Sun*, New York, NY, May 15, 1921, p. 56.
13 Bethlehem Globe, "Indian Who Posed for Indian Head on Buffalo Nickel Greeted by Mayor of Chicago," *Bethlehem Globe*, Bethlehem, PA, June 2, 1921, page unspecified.
14 Philadelphia Inquirer, "Ancient Engine Makes Record Run," *Philadelphia Inquirer*, Philadelphia, PA, October 21, 1927, page unspecified.

15 Indianapolis News, "Blackfoot Indians in City for Visit After Trip to Baltimore," *Indianapolis News*, Indianapolis, IN, October 31, 1927, p. 27.
16 Indianapolis Star, "Blackfeet Tribes Reach City; Plan Two Powwows Today," *Indianapolis Star*, Indianapolis, IN, October 31, 1927, p. 19.

Chapter 8

1 Anonymous, "John Two Guns White Calf" (Wikipedia.org, February 8, 2025), en.wikipedia.org/wiki/John_Two_Guns_White_Calf.
2 Department of Commerce, Bureau of the Census, "Standard Certificate of Death—Two Guns White Calf" (Browning, MT: March 14, 1934), single page.
3 Minneapolis Tribune, "Chief Two Guns White Calf, Buffalo Nickel Indian, Dead," *Minneapolis Tribune*, Minneapolis, MN, March 15, 1934, p. 4.
4 New York Times, "Chief 2-Guns Dies; His Face on Nickel," *New York Times*, New York, NY, March 14, 1934, no page number given.
5 Young, B. W., and McCormack, E. R., *The Dutiful Son: Louis W. Hill—Life in the Shadow of the Empire Builder* (St. Paul, MN: Ramsey County Historical Society, 2010), various pages.
6 Sioux City Journal, "Two Guns White Calf," *Sioux City Journal*, Sioux City, IA, March 18, 1934, p. 4.
7 Peterson, L. L., *Blackfeet John L. "Cutapuis" Clarke and The Silent Call of Glacier National Park* (Helena, MT: Montana Historical Society, 2019), pp. 205-207.
8 Estes, R., "John Two Guns White Calf" *Native Heritage Project* (nativeheritageproject.com/2012/05/21/john-two-guns-white-calf/, 2012).
9 Djuff, R., and Morrison, C., *Glacier's Historic Hotels and Chalets: View with a Room* (Helena, MT: Farcountry Press, 2001), p. 32.
10 Kansas City Public Library, "Portrait of Chief Two Guns White Calf" (Kansas City, MO: Kansas City Public Library), undated, kclibrary.org/art-objects/portrait-chief-two-guns-white-calf.

BIBLIOGRAPHY

Anonymous, "Chief 2-Guns Dies; His Face on Nickel," *The New York Times,* New York, NY, March 14, 1934

Anonymous, "John Two Guns White Calf" (Wikipedia.org, February 8, 2025), en.wikipedia.org/wiki/John_Two_Guns_White_Calf

The Blackfoot Gallery Committee, *The Story of the Blackfoot People: Niitsitapiisinni* (Buffalo, NY: Firefly Books, 2013)

Boileau, T. I., and Boileau, M., "Joe Scheuerle: Modest Man with Friendly Palette," *Montana, The Magazine of Western History*, Vol. 21 No. 4 (Helena, MT: Montana Historical Society, 1971)

Bottomly-O'looney, J., "Sitting Proud: The Indian Portraits of Joseph Scheuerle," *Montana, The Magazine of Western History*, Vol. 58 No. 3 (Helena, MT: Montana Historical Society, 2008)

Butler, D. R., *The Civilian Conservation Corps in Glacier National Park, Montana* (Charleston, SC: America Through Time, 2022)

Butler, D. R., *Early Photographers of Glacier National Park* (Charleston, SC: America Through Time, 2022)

Butler, D. R., *Pioneering Women of Glacier National Park* (Charleston, SC: Fonthill Media, 2023)

Butler, D. R., *Cowboy Artist Charlie Russell and Glacier National Park* (Charleston, SC: Fonthill Media, 2024)

Cahill, C. D., "The Indian Princess Who Wasn't There: The Strange Case of Dawn Mist," Chapter 5 in *Recasting the Vote: How Women of Color Transformed the Suffrage Movement* (Chapel Hill, NC: The University of North Carolina Press, 2020)

Carlson, C. A., "'Uniquely American': The Great Northern Railway, the Blackfeet, and the Creation of a National Identity in Glacier National Park, 1910–1935" (St. Cloud, MN: Department of History, St. Cloud State University Culminating Projects in History 23, repository.stcloudstate.edu/hist_etds/23, 2014)

Cincinnati Art Galleries, *Joseph Scheuerle and His Indian Gallery* (Cincinnati, OH: Cincinnati Art Galleries, 2000)

Department of Commerce, Bureau of the Census, "Standard Certificate of Death—Two Guns White Calf" (Browning, MT: March 14, 1934)

Diettert, G. A., *Grinnell's Glacier: George Bird Grinnell and the Founding of Glacier National Park* (Missoula, MT: Mountain Press Publishing Company, 1992)

Djuff, R., and Morrison, C., *Glacier's Historic Hotels and Chalets: View with a Room* (Helena, MT: Farcountry Press, 2001)

Estes, R., "John Two Guns White Calf," *Native Heritage Project* (nativeheritageproject.com/2012/05/21/john-two-guns-white-calf/, 2012)

Ewers, J. C., *The Story of the Blackfeet* (Lawrence, KS: U.S. Department of the Interior, Branch of Education, Bureau of Indian Affairs, 1944)

Farr, W. E., *The Reservation Blackfeet, 1882–1945: A Photographic History of Cultural Survival* (Seattle, WA: University of Washington Press, 1984, paperback ed. 1986)

Farr, W. E., *Julius Seyler and the Blackfeet: An Impressionist at Glacier National Park* (Norman, OK: University of Oklahoma Press, 2009)

Flandrau, G., *The Story of Marias Pass* (St. Paul, MN: Great Northern Railway, 1925)

Glacier Park Foundation, *A Historical Handbook for the Employees of Glacier Park Lodge* (St. Paul, MN: Glacier Park Foundation, 2016)

Glacier Park Hotel Company, *Picture Writing by the Blackfeet Indians in Glacier Park Hotels* (Glacier Park, MT: Glacier Park Hotel Company, *circa* 1915)

Grafe, S.L. (ed.), *Lanterns on the Prairie: The Blackfeet Photographs of Walter McClintock* (Norman, OK: University of Oklahoma Press, 2009)

Great Northern Railway, *Blackfeet Indians of Glacier National Park* (St. Paul, MN: Great Northern Railway, 1914)

Great Northern Railway, *Glacier National Park* (St. Paul, MN: Great Northern Railway, undated, *circa* 1918)

Great Northern Railway, *The Call of the Mountains: Vacations in Glacier National* Park (St. Paul, MN: Great Northern Railway, 1925)

Guthrie, C. W., *All Aboard! For Glacier: The Great Northern Railway and Glacier National Park* (Helena, MT: Farcountry Press, 2004)

Hall, R., *Beneath the Backbone of the World: Blackfoot People and the North American Borderlands, 1720-1877* (Chapel Hill, NC: University of North Carolina Press, 2020)

Hanna, W. L., *Stars Over Montana: Men Who Made Glacier National Park History* (West Glacier, MT: Glacier Natural History Association, 1988)

Hungry Wolf, A., *Good Medicine in Glacier National Park* (Monee, IL: 1973, edition of 2019)

Ivy, T., Gillenwater, E., Kellogg, D., and Moss, E., *A Timeless Legacy: Women Artists of Glacier National Park* (Kalispell, MT: Hockaday Museum of Art, 2015)

Jermunson, D., *Blackfeet and Glacier Park: The Rest of the Story* (Kalispell, MT: Insty-Prints, 2009)

Jones, D. W., *The Great Northern Railway in Marias Pass* (Charleston, SC: Arcadia Publishing, 2017)

Jones, D., *Glacier National Park: The Great Northern Railway Fred Kiser Artographs 1909–1912* (Liberty Lake, WA: Montana Railroads, 2021)

Kansas City Public Library, "Portrait of Chief Two Guns White Calf" (Kansas City, MO: Kansas City Public Library), undated, kclibrary.org/art-objects/portrait-chief-two-guns-white-calf

Kushner, M. S., *The Art of Winold Reiss: An Immigrant Modernist* (New York City, NY: New York Historical Society Museum and Library, 2021)

Lapier, R. R., and Beck, D. R. M., *City Indian: Native American Activism in Chicago, 1893–1934* (Lincoln, NE: University of Nebraska Press, 2015)

Laut, A. C., *The Blazed Trail of the Old Frontier* (New York, NY: Robert M. McBride & Company, 1926)

Laut, A. C., *Enchanted Trails of Glacier Park* (New York, NY: Robert M. McBride & Company, 1926)

Lawrence, E. R., *Alone with the Past: The Life and Photographic Art of Roland W. Reed* (Afton, MN: Afton Press, 2012)

Linderman, F. B., *Out of the North: A Brief Historical Sketch of the Blackfeet Indian Tribe* (St. Paul, MN: Great Northern Railway Co., 1935, reprinted 1947)

McClintock, W., *The Old North Trail: Life, Legends and Religion of the Blackfeet Indians* (Lincoln, NE: University of Nebraska Press, 1968 edition reproduced from the 1920 first edition)

Minneapolis Tribune, "Chief Two Guns White Calf, Buffalo Nickel Indian, Dead," *Minneapolis Tribune*, Minneapolis, MN, March 15, 1934

Montana Historical Society, *Blackfeet Man: James Willard Schultz* (Helena, MT: Montana Historical Society, 1961)

Moylan, B., *Glacier's Grandest: A Pictorial History of the Hotels and Chalets of Glacier National Park* (Missoula, MT: Pictorial Histories Publishing Company, Inc., 1995)

Museum of the Plains Indian, *Connections: The Blackfeet and Winold Reiss* (Browning, MT: Museum of the Plains Indian, iacbmuseums-viewingroom.exhibit-e.art/viewing-room/connections the-blackfeet-and-winold-reiss#tab:slideshow;tab-1:thumbnails, undated)

New York Times, "Chief 2-Guns Dies; His Face on Nickel," *New York Times*, New York, NY, March 14, 1934

Peterson, L. L., "The Call of the Mountains: Louis Hill and Glacier National Park," *Russell's West, The C.M. Russell Museum Magazine* (Great Falls, MT: C.M. Russell Museum, 2002)

Peterson, L. L., *The Call of the Mountains: The Artists of Glacier National Park* (Tucson, AZ: Settlers West Galleries, 2002)

Peterson, L. L., *John Fery: Artist of Glacier National Park & the American West* (Hayden, ID: The Coeur d' Alene Art Auction, 2015)

Peterson, L. L., *Blackfeet John L. "Cutapuis" Clarke and The Silent Call of Glacier National Park* (Helena, MT: Montana Historical Society, 2019)

Peterson, L. L., *Edward S. Curtis: Printing the Legends—Looking at Shadows in a West Lit Only by Fire* (Helena, MT: Sweetgrass Books, 2024)

Raczka, P., *Winold Reiss Portraits of the Races* (Great Falls, MT: C.M. Russell Museum, 1986)

Rinehart, M. R., *Through Glacier Park: Seeing America First with Howard Eaton* (Boston, MA: Houghton Mifflin and Company, 1916)

Rinehart, M. R., Tenting To-night: A Chronical of Sport and Adventure in Glacier Park and the Cascade Mountains (Boston, MA: Houghton Mifflin Company, 1918)

Ruby, J., "Photographs of the Piegan by Roland Reed (Photo Essay)," *Studies in Visual Communication*, Vol. 7 No. 1 (Philadelphia, PA: University of Pennsylvania, 1981)

Schultz, J. W., *My Life as an Indian* (Greenwich, CT: Fawcett Publications, Inc., reprint of book published by Forest and Stream Magazine, 1907)

Schultz, J. W., *Blackfeet Tales of Glacier National Park* (Boston, MA: Houghton Mifflin Company, 1916)

Schutz, L., "The Blackfoot Indians in New York City: Historic Photos from the Museum of the City of New York," *HuffPost*, (www.huffpost.com/entry/the-blackfoot-indians-in_b_847936, 2011)

Scriver, B., *The Blackfeet: Artists of the Northern Plains: the Scriver Collection of Blackfeet Indian Artifacts and Related Objects, 1894–1990* (Kansas City, MO: The Lowell Press, Inc., 1990)

Sioux City Journal, "Two Guns White Calf," *Sioux City Journal*, Sioux City, IA, March 18, 1934

Taliaferro, J., *Grinnell: America's Environmental Pioneer and His Restless Drive to Save the West* (New York City, NY: Liveright Publishing Corporation, 2019)

Thompson, M., *High Trails of Glacier National Park* (Caldwell, ID: The Caxton Printers, Ltd., 1936)

Thompson, S., Kootenai Culture Committee, and Pikunni Traditional Association, *People Before the Park: The Kootenai and Blackfeet Before Glacier National Park* (Helena, MT: Montana Historical Society Press, 2015)

U.S. Department of the Interior, *Glacier National Park* (Washington, DC: Department of the Interior, *circa* 1916)

Wood, C. R., *Lines West: Great Northern* (Burbank, CA: Superior Publishing Company, 1967)

Wyckoff, W., and Dilsaver, L. M., "Promotional Imagery of Glacier National Park," *The Geographical Review*, Vol. 87 No. 1 (New York, NY: American Geographical Society, 1997)

Young, B. W., and McCormack, E. R., *The Dutiful Son: Louis W. Hill—Life in the Shadow of the Empire Builder* (St. Paul, MN: Ramsey County Historical Society, 2010)